Judith Baker Montano's
Essential Stitch Guide

A Source Book of Inspiration

The Best of *Elegant Stitches* & *Floral Stitches*

Judith Baker Montano

C&T PUBLISHING

Text, photography, and artwork copyright © 2016 by Judith Baker Montano

Publisher: Amy Marson

Creative Director: Gailen Runge

Art Director/Cover Designer: Kristy Zacharias

Editor: Lynn Koolish

Technical Editor: Helen Frost

Book Design: Page+Pixel

Production Coordinator: Zinnia Heinzmann

Production Editor: Joanna Burgarino

Illustrators: Judith Baker Montano,
Michaela Carr, Ginny Coull, Mary Flynn,
Tim Manibusan, Alan McKorkle,
Kirstie L. Pettersen, and Richard Sheppard

Photography by Judith Baker Montano,
unless otherwise noted

Published by C&T Publishing, Inc., P.O. Box 1456, Lafayette, CA 94549

Library of Congress Cataloging-in-Publication Data

Montano, Judith Baker, 1945- author.

Judith Baker Montano's essential stitch guide : a source book of inspiration-the best of elegant stitches & floral stitches / Judith Baker Montano.

    pages cm

Includes bibliographical references and index.

ISBN 978-1-61745-077-8 (soft cover)

1. Embroidery--Patterns. 2. Stitches (Sewing) I. Title. II. Title: Essential stitch guide.

TT773.M573 2016

746.44'041--dc23

2015027785

Printed in China

10 9 8 7 6

CONTENTS

SILK RIBBON STITCHES 91

Dedication

This book is dedicated to my wonderful students and readers. Thank you for your support and friendship.

INTRODUCTION

Embroidery. The word conjures up so many memories for me: my grandmother finishing up yet another set of tea towels, one for each day of the week; the gift of a chain-stitch horse head, made by my daughter in her seventh grade home economics class; the silk ribbon flowers on my wedding dress still hanging in the closet; the silver crane worked in silk by a Japanese student, shyly handed to me in Tokyo, Japan; happily embroidering flowers on denim overalls for my granddaughter Kelse seventeen years ago and now for my youngest granddaughter, Paloma. All those wonderful memories are woven around embroidery.

Thanks to the embroidery and quilting world, I have a wonderful career as a teacher, designer, and fiber artist. It has taken me around the world and opened so many doors. I've found that women and men from all walks of life enjoy needlework. I've seen students around the world come together to enjoy the common denominator of cloth, needle, and thread. I've taught classes where more than ten different languages were spoken and yet everyone understood the language of needlework. Whether you use embroidery to enhance the beauty of a fabric, to create an original work of art, or to simply relax from a busy work schedule, it is a technique that is here to stay— one that brings great satisfaction and pleasure.

I could have used a good stitch book in the beginning because I really struggled with the stitches. I used the Coats & Clark pamphlet *100 Embroidery Stitches* to learn the basic stitches, but because I am dyslexic it was very difficult to follow the instructions. That's why years later I wrote the embroidery stitch books *Elegant Stitches* and *Floral Stitches.* Now I am combining them into one concise stitch dictionary. It is a basic reference book of categorized stitches that you can easily work in thread, yarn, or ribbon. I have included photographs, clear instructions, and precise diagrams.

You will also find:

- Embroidery basics including needles, fabrics, and supplies

- Advice for left-handed stitchers

- Crazy-quilt stitch combinations

- Free-form embroidery stitches

GETTING STARTED
WITH THE BASICS

Embroidery is a very rewarding art. It will give you years of enjoyment, but like any hobby or craft, it takes practice and patience. Start with the proper tools and materials and get to know their uses.

FABRICS

Many fabric types will provide interesting and varied backgrounds that can enhance the needlework and not overshadow it. Add an extra 2″ to the fabric measurement to aid in the handling and stretching of the fabric prior to stitching. Always test to make sure the base is sturdy enough to act as a background for your design.

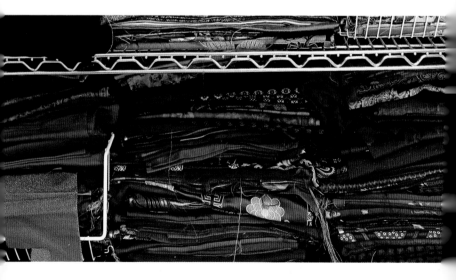

- Is the fabric appropriate for the subject matter?

- How much wear and tear will it receive?

- Will the threads, yarn, or ribbon work up properly on the fabric selected?

Aida	Cross-stitch fabric with holes set at a definite spacing. Use the high count (more holes to an inch) for backgrounds.
Canvas for Needlepoint or Cross-Stitch	These specialty fabrics come in different fibers (cotton or linen); the holes are spaced according to size (number of threads to the inch).
Cotton, Polyester, Linen, Shantung	Medium-weight fabrics that can support many types of embroidery.
Knit, Loosely Woven Fabric	Some of these loose weaves may need a stable fabric on the back to hold the stitches in place.
Leather and Ultrasuede	Have a stiletto ready because every hole must be punched due to the thickness of these materials.
Lightweight Silk, Organza, Batiste	These are delicate fabrics and may need a bottom layer to stabilize them. Keep the thread and ribbon ends well concealed because they may show through such delicate fabrics.
Moiré	Fabric with a watermark design that gives a Victorian, old-fashioned look.
Muslin	Has a coarser finish but a good choice; gives an informal feel, a country look.
Satin	Elegant, formal fabric with a smooth surface. Test to make sure water doesn't eliminate the shine; good for fancy work associated with crazy quilting.
Plush, Velvet	An old-fashioned-looking fabric; the texture provides added depth. Always choose velvet with a crushed or low nap. Use stitches that will sit up on the fabric or the stitches may get lost in the texture of the fabric.
Silk	Always an excellent choice. It can be shiny, matte, or textured; a multipurpose fabric.
Taffeta, Shot Cloth	These fabrics take on an old-fashioned Victorian look that's good for fancy work associated with crazy quilting.
Wool	Use stitches that will sit up on the fabric or the stitches may get lost in the texture of the fabric.

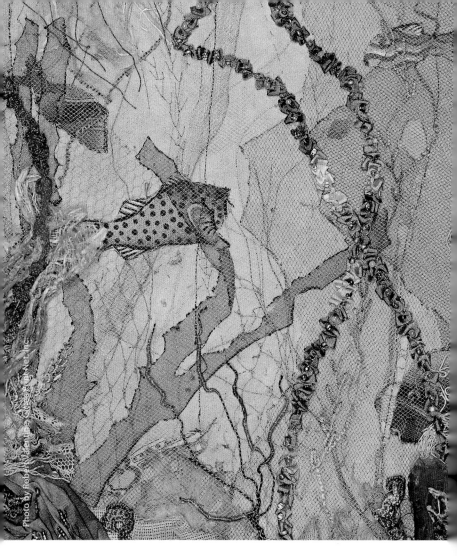

OVERLAYS

Use sheer fabrics as overlays to create interesting and unusual effects for the background. By cutting or burning the pieces into unusual shapes, you can create a feeling of depth and shadow. By layering several sheer fabrics and letting the cut or burned shapes overlap in places, you can create light and dark areas for visual interest. A painted background may be muted with sheer overlays to create a hazy effect. I use this method to create underwater scenes.

Always have a good variety of sheer fabrics on hand. Look for organza, netting, tulle, and batiste. Many of these fabrics now come in a wrinkled state and some have glitter.

Needles

NEEDLE	SIZES	USAGE
Beading A very fine, long needle with a tiny eye used strictly for beading	#10–#15; I recommend a #10	The length aids in loading the needle with beads. Sharps beading needles are short and used for picking up one bead at a time.
Betweens (quilting) A short, fine needle with a round eye	#5–#12	Use for quilting and fine hand sewing.
Chenille A long-eyed needle with a sharp point	#18–#24	Use for working heavy threads, fabrics, and silk ribbon embroidery.
Crewel embroidery A sharp needle with a long, oval eye	#1–#10	Use for fine to medium surfaces.
Darner A long-eyed needle with a sharp point	Keep sizes #14–#18 on hand	Use for assembly work, wool darning, and working with heavy threads and fabrics.
Millinery (straw needle) A long, narrow needle, the same thickness from end to end, with a small, round eye	#1–#11	Excellent for making French knots.
Sharps A short, fine, strong, round-eyed needle	Common sizes are #10, #11, and #12	Excellent for fine embroidery and hand sewing.
Tapestry A large oval-eyed needle with a rounded point	#13–#26	Use for working pulled and drawn work and silk ribbon embroidery.

THREADS

The choice of thread is always governed by your choice of fabric and the project in mind. Experiment with different threads and yarns to find what works best with various types of fabrics.

Brazilian embroidery thread	A rayon, twisted embroidery thread with a good sheen; use short lengths as it tends to knot up.
Coton á Broder	A single, highly twisted thread with a shiny finish.
Crewel Yarns	A very fine three-stranded wool; the strands can be separated and used singly.
Filo-Floss	A soft, loosely twisted, six-stranded silk thread; it can be separated to use singly or in varying multiple strands.
Linen	A highly twisted, single thread that's very strong and has a slight sheen.
Marlett	A shiny, viscose thread; comes in loose strands and can be separated for finer work.
Metallic	Any thread with glitter and shine is referred to as a metallic.
Natesh	A rayon thread with a wonderful sheen; double it for Victorian crazy-quilt stitching.
Perle cotton	A single thread with a sharply defined twist and low luster; sizes 3, 5, and 8 (the thinnest).
Persian wool	A three-stranded wool, thicker than crewel but thinner than tapestry, that can be easily separated use for textural work.
Silk buttonhole twist	Three strands of tightly twisted silk threads in a fine cord with a soft sheen.
Silk ribbon	A soft pliable silk ribbon that comes in a large range of colors, variegations, and widths; used for embroidery and surface embellishment.
Silk sewing thread	A single strand of very fine thread that's used for heirloom sewing.
Soie d'Algere	A seven-stranded silk thread that can be separated or used as is.
Stranded embroidery floss	A six- to fourteen-stranded cotton or silk thread that separates to be used one strand at a time or in multiples.
Tapestry wool	A thick yarn traditionally used for needlepoint.
Ver à Soie	A twisted silk thread similar to buttonhole twist.

TECHNIQUES

Embroidery

Think of the stitches you've learned over the years and choose those that will best support your floral design. Remember that your fabric is like a painter's canvas, and you are the artist. Your threads and yarn are your paints. Use a selection of threads and yarns with a variety of widths and textures.

Silk-Ribbon Embroidery

Silk-ribbon embroidery uses traditional embroidery stitches that add dimension and texture. It is a marvelous medium for floral designs. The traditional width is 4mm, and you must use either a chenille or a tapestry needle to execute the stitches. Silk ribbon is wonderful to mix with other embroidery techniques.

The secret to good ribbon embroidery is to keep the stitches loose but controlled. With some stitches it is very important to keep the ribbon flat. Silk-ribbon embroidery is dimensional and fast. Here are a few tips to make your stitching easy and successful.

Threading the Ribbon: Remember, silk ribbon is delicate and will fray on the edges. Use a short length (12˝–16˝) and a needle with a larger eye.

Needle Eye Lock: Thread the ribbon through the eye of the needle. Pierce one end of the ribbon (directly in the center and ¼″ from the end) with the point of the needle. Pull the long end of the ribbon and lock it into the eye of the needle.

Soft Knot: To make the needle eye lock, grasp the end of the ribbon and then form a circle with the end of the ribbon and the point of the needle (A). Pierce the bottom end of the ribbon with a short running stitch (B). Pull the needle and ribbon through the running stitch to form a soft knot.

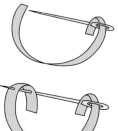

Ribbon Manipulation: Learn to use the ribbon properly. If it is pulled too tight or twisted too much, it will just look like a heavy thread. Keep the ribbon length short, as it is easier to manipulate. Use your free thumb to hold the ribbon flat against the fabric because most stitches depend on the ribbon being flat. Keep your thumb in place while you stitch and tighten the ribbon over the thumb. This will remove any twists. A large needle, toothpick, or knitting stitch holder can be used instead of your thumb.

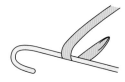

Adjusting the Ribbon: Sometimes the ribbon will fold up on itself as it passes through the fabric; then it has to be adjusted so the full width of the ribbon shows. Hold the ribbon flat under the free thumb and slide the needle under the ribbon. Then gently slide the needle back and forth, from the thumb to the needle hole in the fabric.

Correct Needles: Use a chenille needle when piercing through fabric and a tapestry needle for wrapping or whipping. Tightly woven and heavier fabrics call for a larger needle eye. This helps to create a larger hole that enables the ribbon to pass through without distress.

Punchneedle Embroidery

Always use a tight, even-weave fabric for punchneedle embroidery, making sure the fabric is drum-tight in the hoop. The beauty of this technique is that the loops can be very long or short and can be sheared for a velour look. Punchneedle embroidery can be mixed with other techniques to create visual interest.

Start out with a simple design and a medium needle that takes up to three strands of floss. Keep the fabric drum-tight in an embroidery hoop or else the stitches will not hold.

Remember that the design is punched from the back, so the pattern must show on the back. The front design will be opposite of the back. Make sure the design is facing the proper direction!

1. Closely examine the needle. On the pointed end, one side is open and cut at an angle. On the other end is a small eye. The open, slanted side must always face the same direction as you are stitching. The thread must come up at the top and through the eye. Hold the

needle like a pencil. Relax your hand and do not hold it too tight. Make sure the thread coming out of the end of the handle is not obstructed.

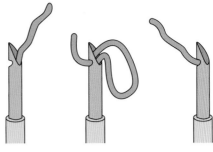

Threading up the punchneedle

tips

- If you need to remove stitches, simply pull them out. Realign the fabric threads by scratching over the surface with your fingernail.

- Do not reuse the thread— cut this portion off.

- Outline the design in a darker shade of thread to highlight it, and fill in with various colors and shades.

- Punch in rows of punch-needle embroidery side by side and do not overcrowd. For best results, the rows should follow the contour of the shape being filled.

2. Insert the needle, at the same 70° angle as the slanted side of the needle, into the fabric. Push it all the way down until the gauge stops it. Lift the needle back to the surface but do not lift it off of the surface. Drag it along the next stitch, about ⅟32″ (1mm), and repeat. Think of it as punch, drag, punch, drag! Do not lift the needle off of the surface. If you do, the stitches will be messy with skipped loops. After the thread is used up, cut it off flush at the back.

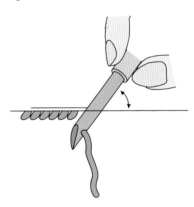

Inserting the punchneedle in fabric

As with any other technique, punchneedle embroidery requires practice. With a bit of practice, it is easy to get the stitches small and even. Adjust the gauges on the punchneedle for loops or various depths.

Cross-Stitch and Needlepoint

To transfer designs or graphs for cross-stitch or needlepoint, I use a lightbox and graph paper placed over a watercolor design. (Be sure to use the correct size of graph paper!) Then I color it in with watercolor pencils. You can also use plastic graph overlays, which can be purchased from craft and needlework stores. Place the plastic graph over the watercolor design and then work it onto the chosen fabric. You can also use computer programs to scan your designs and produce a professional chart!

Beads

A chart for beads is very similar to a cross-stitch chart. Once again, I make a graph and work my beads according to color. I prefer to use beads for highlights, to indicate flower stamens, or to form fantasy shapes.

Mixed Media

Needlework techniques of all types can be used to create original and exciting projects. Now is the time to think back on what you've learned over the years from those classes, books, and techniques. Don't be afraid to combine them. Play around with color and shading. Relax and try different combinations until you come up with a pleasing design.

HOOPS

Using a hoop prevents the stitches from pulling too tightly and the base fabric from wrinkling. A hoop in which your thumb and fingers reach comfortably to the middle seems to be the best (5″–6″). Hoops come in metal, plastic, and wood. A wooden hoop with the inner circle wrapped in yarn holds well and is especially useful when stitching velvet or high-napped fabrics.

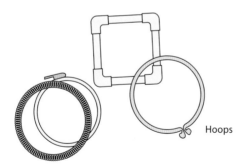

Hoops

1. Insert the fabric into the hoop by placing the area to be embroidered over the inner ring.

2. Align the fabric so the grain is straight and the surface is smooth.

3. Add the top circle and adjust the tension screw if needed.

Always remove your work from the hoop when not embroidering so the fabric isn't marked or creased.

tip

If odd shapes are problematic, sew the shape onto a large square of support fabric first, basting the shape in place with small running stitches. Insert into the hoop. Working from the wrong side of the fabric, cut away the support fabric from inside the odd shape. The fabric is now ready for embroidery work.

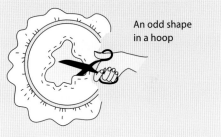
An odd shape in a hoop

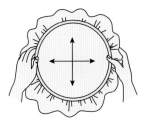
Adjusting fabric in the hoop

FRAMES

Used for large pieces of embroidery, frames keep the fabric taut and even during stitching. The basic frame consists of two rollers (top and bottom) that have strips of tape or canvas webbing added across the bar length. To support the base fabric, first zigzag stitch a ½″ hem on the edges. A base that is a fine fabric almost always requires support for the edges; try stitching bias tape or attaching strips of support fabric to the edges. The overall stitching area depends on the length of the rollers and the length of the side supports.

Roller frame

1. Mark the center of both rollers and the top and bottom edges of the base fabric.

2. Attach the edges of the fabric to the tape or canvas strips on the rollers using lacing stitches.

3. Match the center points and work outward from the center.

4. Roll any excess fabric around one roller.

The flat-sided supports hold the rollers in place with pegs or screws.

5. Attach the flat-sided supports and then roll the bars to stretch the fabric.

6. Using strong thread, lace the fabric edges evenly to the flat side supports. Tighten the lace on each side and knot the thread ends firmly.

Lacing the frame

An added benefit to a frame is that it can be secured on a stand, allowing the needle-worker to use both hands while working the stitches.

Frame on stand

SMALL SEWING TOOLS

Be sure to have small items such as thimbles, needles, straight pins, glue stick, ruler, tweezers, scissors, pencils, and markers close at hand. There is nothing worse than having to search for sewing tools.

Thimbles: Many types of thimbles are available on the market. Just make sure the thimble fits snugly over the middle finger of your stitching hand. You need the small indentations on the tip to hold and guide the needle into place, as well as to protect your fingers!

Scissors: Many different types of scissors are available, and they are an investment. Test them to be sure they fit your hand and fingers. Make sure to have a variety of scissors nearby. Don't be tempted to use those prized embroidery scissors for anything else but threads!

- *Embroidery scissors:* These small scissors come in many pleasing shapes and sizes. Make sure they are sharp and strong with pointed blades for precise cutting. Have more than one pair for multiple projects.

- *Cloth scissors:* Invest in one good pair of 8″–10″ shears for cutting fabric. Keep them sharpened, oiled, and stored with tip guards.

- *Utility Scissors:* You will always need scissors for cutting paper and template plastic.

Rulers: Make sure to have small see-through rulers as well as yardsticks and tape measures. Remember the adage: "Measure twice and cut once!"

Thread Tweezers: I use my thread tweezers so many times in fine embroidery work. Make sure the tips are long and pointed.

Pencils and Pens: I have a big variety of pencils on my work table. Always use a light hand when using any pencil or pen! When in doubt, test on paper or fabric to avoid tragedies.

- *Water-erasable pens:* Use a very light hand with these pens. As you stitch, make sure that the embroidered stitches cover all the marks. Erase the marks from the fabric with cold water. I use a Q-tip or a water brush to remove the lines.

- *Fade-away pens:* Again, use a very light hand and be aware that the marks will fade after 24 hours.

- *White or silver pencils:* Use these pencils on dark fabrics and keep a sharp point on them.

- *Chaco markers:* These markers use powder in a tube that is distributed with a small wheel at the base; the chalk comes in many colors.

Transferring Designs

Needlework designs can be found in magazines, coloring books, and design books, but they must be transferred to the base fabric in order to start.

Important! *Either use your own designs or make sure that any design to take from any other source is copyright free.*

Lightbox: A lightbox can save many hours.

1. Trace your pattern onto tracing paper, making sure the lines are clear and dark.

2. Place the traced pattern on the lightbox and place the base fabric over the paper.

3. Trace the outlines with chalk, a light pencil, or a water-erasable pen.

tip

A natural lightbox is as close as your window.

Dressmaker's Carbon Paper: Best suited for smooth fabrics.

1. Trace the design on the paper.

2. Place the paper carbon side down on the fabric.

3. Redraw the design with a pencil or ball-point pen.

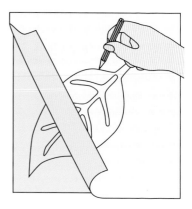

Carbon trace

Basting through Tissue Paper:
Use for high-napped fabrics
such as plush, velvet, or wool.

1. Pin the tissue paper (with the outline pattern) onto the fabric.

2. Outline the design with small running stitches.

3. Tear away the paper.

Remove the basting after the embroidery is completed.

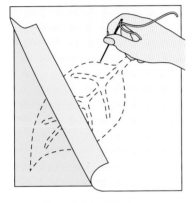

Basting through tissue paper

Direct Transfer Method: Use with fine transparent fabrics such as lawn, organdy, nylon, or silk. Directly trace the embroidery design onto the fabric using a pencil or pen made for marking fabrics.

Iron-on Transfers: An easy transfer method. Preprinted designs are available, or you can make your own using an iron-on transfer product.

Use a hot iron to imprint the design onto your base fabric, but remember that the design reverses when applied! Always test on a sample piece of cloth first; some synthetic fabrics won't take the transfer.

Iron-on Transfer Pencils:
Note that this method of transfer also reverses the design.

1. Trace the design onto tracing paper using these special pencils.

2. Place the traced design face-down on the base fabric.

3. Iron onto the fabric.

ENLARGING AND REDUCING DESIGNS

Patterns are easily reduced or enlarged, and help is only as far away as your nearest computer or copy machine. If this isn't possible, simply use the grid method (below).

1. Start by tracing your original design onto paper and enclose it in a rectangle. Place the traced design in the bottom corner of a large sheet of paper. Figure A

2. Working from a right-angle corner (A), draw a diagonal line through the opposite corner of the design to the edge of the paper (B).

3. Mark the desired height of the new design along the Y axis to (Y).

4. Extend a horizontal line from point Y to the diagonal line (B).

5. Make a vertical line from point B to the X axis (X).

6. Divide the original design into squares to form an overall grid.

7. Mark off the large rectangle with the same number of squares.

8. Draw each design line from the small grid to the large squares. Figure B

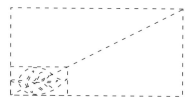

A. Setting up to enlarge

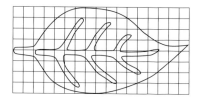

B. Enlarging using a grid

WASHING FINISHED WORK

1. Use cold water and pure soap flakes.

2. Gently squeeze any excess water from the fabric.

3. Rinse thoroughly.

4. Roll into a large terry towel and press to remove excess moisture.

5. Leave until partially dry before blocking and pressing.

Judith Baker Montano's Essential Stitch Guide

BLOCKING AND PRESSING

After the finished work is washed:

1. Measure a piece of graph paper the same size as the base fabric.

2. Place the fabric right side up on the paper and, using the grid lines, pull the fabric into shape. Pin in position with rust-proof push pins.

3. Cover the fabric with a damp cloth or acid-free tissue paper and leave to dry.

If the embroidery is hard to block or blocking isn't required, place it right side down on a well-padded board (use toweling for ribbon work) and press lightly using a damp pressing cloth. Do not flatten the embroidery.

ADDING HIGHLIGHTS

Don't be afraid to collage different techniques and materials together. After you've finished the embroidery, it may look a bit dull or sparse. Adding beads, tiny buttons, or metal findings may be the pièce de résistance to complete your work. Be sure to keep these highlights in proportion to your work.

Beads: Small seed beads add sparkle and visual beauty to embroidery. Use them to fill in the centers of flowers or to act as individual buds. Use Nymo beading thread for sewing them in place; this thread will not deteriorate with time or cleaning, and it is virtually invisible within the embroidery.

Buttons: Keep the button size in proportion to the embroidery. Small mother-of-pearl buttons are pretty with soft pastel work. Antique buttons are better with crazy-quilt stitching.

Metal findings: Small brass and silver doodads come in a huge variety of shapes and subjects. Perhaps a little bee or a butterfly will add a special highlight to your creation. Have fun with these additions.

- Before starting a project, test your threads, yarns, and ribbons for colorfastness: Place short lengths over the edge of a glass filled with water. Let the ends dangle into the water. Leave them for ten minutes; then remove and place them between white paper towels. Press with your fingers or an iron. Open the towels and check for color stains.

- Always make a small trial piece to test the threads, stitches, and fabric itself.

- Cut more fabric than you will need. The rule of thumb is 2″ extra all around.

- Avoid knots on the back of your finished work, because they create bumps that show up as shiny spots when pressed. When possible, run the starting end of the thread through the fabric under the area to be worked. Finish on the wrong side by running the end under the stitches just worked.

- Cut clothing pattern pieces larger than needed if they are to be embellished. This helps when inserting the fabric in the hoop or frame. After construction of the garment, work some of the embroidery over the seamlines for a more professional look.

- Always press your finished work on a padded board. Press from the wrong side with a damp pressing cloth. If you have to press silk ribbon work, use a steam iron and a terry towel for padding.

Hover the iron above the fabric and set the steam on high. Puff-press from the back and shake out.

STORING TOOLS AND MATERIALS

Nothing is more frustrating than searching for tools or materials when you are in the middle of a project. I speak from great experience! Here are a few suggestions for organizing your workroom or classroom.

- Store ribbons and threads in see-through containers or wrap them on wooden thread winders. I loop my threads on large wooden rings and hang them from pegs. Just get your materials out where they are visible and readily available.

- Keep several needle cases, loaded with a wide variety of needles, on hand. Keep the main one in your workspace and keep one in every project bag.

- Invest in several embroidery scissors so that you have a pair in the workspace and with each project.

- Pull all the ribbons, threads, fabrics, and tools necessary for a project, and then keep them in one container. I use a large serving tray or trays. Use plastic boxes or baskets—whatever will help keep your project supplies organized.

- If you are traveling, designate a special carrier as a needlework travel bag. Make sure it has sections to hold ribbon, thread, fabrics, and tools, plus a pocket to keep your project clean and safe.

- Purchase a small pillowcase or make one of calico (muslin). Store your unfinished projects in these little pillowcases to keep your work clean and neat.

METRIC CONVERSIONS

The old adage "measure twice and cut once" is so true. Below is a ruler with both inches and centimeters and a conversion chart to help simplify the mystery of inches, millimeters, centimeters, and meters.

In the metric system, everything is done in multiples of ten. I have memorized this little verse for myself:

There are 10 millimeters in 1 centimeter and 100 millimeters in 10 centimeters

and 100 centimeters in 1 meter. There are 10 centimeters in 3.93 inches and

1 meter equals 39.3 inches.

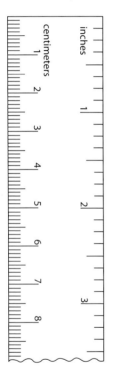

LENGTH CONVERSIONS

INCHES	MILLIMETERS	CENTIMETERS
1/16″	1.6mm	
1/8″	3mm	
1/4″	6.3mm	
1/2″	12.7mm	
3/4″	19mm	
1″	25.4mm	2.54cm
6″		15.24cm
12″		30.48cm
39.37″		100.00cm (1 meter)

FEET	YARDS	METERS
1′		0.30m
2′		0.61m
3′	1 yard	0.91m
6′	2 yards	1.83m

DESIGN IDEAS

Over the years I have tried many different crafts. I keep books on a variety of subjects for ideas and patterns in my mixed-media pieces. I also keep magazines, clippings, photos, and journals, filed by category for easy reference. The following designing steps for "Floral Steps" will inspire and get you thinking of ways to mix techniques and ideas.

Designing Floral Steps

Several years ago while staying at a lodge in Tasmania, Australia, I took a photograph of beautiful stone garden steps. I chose to use it as the centerpiece for a floral needlework project.

First I made a copy of the photograph and picked out several floral clippings. I decided on a 5″ × 7″ size and made a rough sketch. I then trimmed several of the clippings, picking out special floral shapes. I had more than I would need, but that gave me choices. Some of you will be afraid to try this, but relax—you are simply trying out different design ideas.

I cut out the stone steps and placed them onto a large sheet of paper. I moved the floral shapes around the steps, trying out different placements. When I decided on the design, I glued everything in place with a glue stick.

With tracing paper, pencil, and a lightbox, I traced my design. When I was happy with the tracing, I inked it in with a Sharpie permanent marker. I then taped the traced paper design to the lightbox and traced the design onto watercolor paper with a pencil. After I was happy with the pencil lines, I then inked in the lines with a fine-point Pigma Micron permanent pen. I painted the design onto the watercolor paper for practice and reference.

For the fabric painting I chose a very fine cross-stitch fabric and traced the floral design with a pencil. Last but not least, I retraced the pencil lines with a fine-point Pigma Micron permanent pen. This ink will not run when the watercolor paint is applied. Figure A

I used a framing mat with a 5″ × 7″ opening to trace the outer perimeter onto the fabric with a water- erasable pen. After dampening the chosen fabric, I painted the background with watercolor paint. When it dried (I hurry along the drying with a hair dryer or an iron), I added more color to the floral shapes and the stone steps. After it was completely dried, it was ready for stitching and embellishing. Figure B

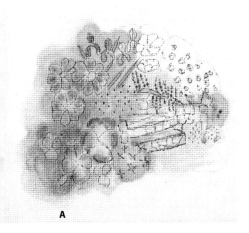

A

B

BACKGROUNDS

Nothing is more important than the background of your intended needleart design. Many things have to be taken into consideration, such as the mood you are trying to create, the contrast, and the workability of the material.

Use color and tone to determine the mood:

- For a soft, feminine look, use light pastel colors on a background of white or cream.

- For an antique and muted look, use dusty colors on a taupe or grayed background.

- For sharp contrast and drama, use jewel tones on black.

Always remember that the background should not overshadow the needlework; it is there as a complement.

Painted Backgrounds

When you look at fabric as a painter's canvas, a whole new avenue of design opens up. For framed pieces, I use all types of paints (acrylic, oil, and watercolor) but prefer watercolor. For anything that may be laundered, I use fabric paints and dyes. I apply these like watercolor washes. I dilute the paint, so I am forced to use several layers to achieve the finished look. Remember that a painted background is the background; your needlework should "float" on top.

Decide on the finished size and cut the fabric at least 2˝ beyond on all sides. Tape or pin the fabric to a wood frame so that it remains taut. Dampen the area you are painting (just as a watercolorist works on wet paper) to ensure the colors blend into each other. The paint will dry to a lighter hue, but be sure it is dry before you dampen and add another layer.

A painted fabric background works best if the base is a natural fiber and of a tight weave. The natural fiber (such as linen, silk, cotton) absorbs and holds the paint; polyesters tend to repel paint. The tighter the weave, the smoother the surface will be. Similar to choosing the rag quality in paper, a more textured surface might be exactly what you are looking for!

Photo Transfers

As technology improves, we see more types of photo transfers. As opposed to those that were stiff and difficult to embroider, the newer applications are soft and pliable. I still prefer the Australian photo method, but it requires a dry-toner copy machine that is becoming outdated (refer to page 45 of *Crazy Quilt Handbook, Revised 3rd Edition*).

Many antique paintings, Victorian ephemera, and photographs are now offered as preprinted designs to embellish. Although the finish is rather stiff, the base is very workable.

Today you can scan artwork with a computer and transfer it onto fabric with a printer either by printing directly onto the fabric or by using an iron-on transfer product. *This does bring up a point of concern: the subject of copyright. Become familiar with the rules of copyright and the restrictions. Always protect yourself and always give credit where credit is due.*

THINK LIKE A PAINTER

The rules for successful needlework are the same as the rules applied to painting. I encourage my students to think of themselves as artists, to think like a painter and observe with a "painter's eye."

Before you start, decide on the mood of the piece—where the light and shadows will fall, the time of day, and the light source. This adds to the mood or feel of your project.

Always remember that light values come forward and dark values recede. Large objects cast shadows. Just as a painter lays down layers of washes and paints, you will do the same with your chosen materials, building from the back to the front of your piece. Painting with paint, fabric, or threads is a backward journey!

A painting or needlework creation has three major sections:

Background	Everything in this area is very far away and small. Use dark colors to show depth or overlays for a hazy quality. Background shapes must be worked in fine threads and small stitches.
Midground	Everything here is of medium proportion. It's the separation between "here" and "way over there." Some midground shapes overlap objects in the background to create a feeling of depth. Work with medium-weight threads and lighter colors.
Foreground	Everything in this area is visible and detailed. Work with heavier threads and in lighter colors to create depth and texture.

Horizon Line

Garden scenes, landscapes, and seascapes require a bit more thought. Along with the background, midground, and foreground is the horizon line (the distinguishing line between sky and land). The viewer's eye will always travel to the horizon line. The horizon

line can be high or low but never in the center, because that is disturbing to the eye. Always put the horizon line above or below the center mark. A high horizon will leave more midground and foreground for more stitching!

V and S Shapes

To make the eye travel within the design, use two painting techniques: the V shape and the S shape. For example, by creating a valley—a V shape—of trees and shrubs for a garden scene (in the center of the V), the viewer will instantly look into the garden area.

The S shape, whether a path, road, or stream, will draw the viewer's eye into the picture. As the eye travels along the S shape, the eye perceives the picture details.

V-shape

S-shape

Water

When working with seascapes or large expanses of water, a few points will make for a more pleasing and realistic picture.

- Large expanses of water always lie in a straight, horizontal line and form the horizon line.

- Smooth, calm water acts as a reflector, or mirror, and the upside-down reflected image needs to be indicated somehow.

- Little inlets and lagoons are shadowed.

- Lakes and rivers are contained by banks of land, so the bank fabric must lie over the water fabric.

The sea and ocean waters roll in and over the beaches, so lay the water material over the beach fabric!

COLOR

Montano Color Chart

Many of my students are hesitant about using color. Their confidence has been eroded over the years, and they've been led to believe that color is some big mystery. I have a simple formula to help overcome these fears. This Montano Color Chart is easy to follow and applies to clothing design, crazy quilting, landscapes, and all types of needlework.

LIGHT	LIGHT MEDIUM	MEDIUM	DARK MEDIUM	DARK
Paint				
Add white to paint	Add a little black to paint	Add a little more black	Add more black	Contrast between colors
Fabric				
Pastel	Light dusty	Medium dusty	Dark dusty	Jewel
Soft	Desert	Worn	Rembrandt	Mardi Gras
Baby	Hazy	Foggy	Antique	Fireworks
Feminine	Old	Storm	Moody	Dramatic
Extenders and Backgrounds				
White	Cream	Dark cream	Black	Black
Cream	Light Gray	Khaki	Dark Gray	
	Taupe		Taupe	
Highlights				
Silver	Silver	Silver	Silver	Silver
	Light gold	Medium gold	Old Gold	Old Gold
				Rust Orange

Light: To create something with lots of light, a painter squirts out the basic colors and then adds lots of titanium white. The colors become very light and soft (red becomes pink, orange becomes peach, purple becomes soft lavender).

Light Medium: To create a desert scene, she adds a bit of black to the white to make gray, then adds this to her basic colors.

Dark Medium: To create something moody, she will simply add more black to the paint in order to darken the piece.

Dark: Think of sharp contrast, lots of drama (perhaps fireworks or neon lights).

Black: Always makes bold colors seem more vibrant.

Fabric: In fabric and thread terms, light becomes pastel, medium becomes dusty, and dark becomes jewel tone. Look through your fabrics and threads to decide what category they belong. Keep in mind that lights come forward and darks recede.

Extenders and Backgrounds: These are colors that will extend your work visually and work well for the background. They always complement and show off your chosen colors in the best possible way.

Highlights: These are colors that will add a bit of sparkle and interest to your work.

Color Wheel

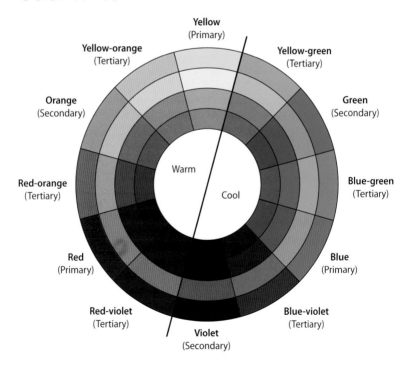

COLOR WHEEL SIMPLIFIED

Invest in a simple color wheel and learn how to use it.
Look at the whole wheel and study the spectrum of colors.
Notice that there is a warm side and a cool side to the
wheel (warm = reds and oranges, cool = blues and greens).

Primary Colors: Red, blue, and yellow are the three primary colors.

Secondary Colors: Combined primary colors produce the three secondary colors: green, violet, and orange (yellow + blue = green; blue + red = violet; red + yellow = orange).

Tertiary Colors: Combining a primary and a secondary color makes a tertiary color. These are yellow green, blue green, blue violet, red violet, red orange, and yellow orange

Complementary Colors: Look for a favorite color on the wheel, and then straight across from it is the complement. For example, the complement of red is green. Choose violet and look across to yellow—once again, complementary colors.

Triad Combination: Three colors set equal distance apart on the color wheel are a triad. In a color wheel are four different triad combinations.

Monochromatic: This is one color and one shade. In order to give monochromatics extra interest, use combinations of shiny, matte, and textured materials.

Analogous Colors: These are neighboring hues that create harmonious combinations.

FRAMING IDEAS

Framing can become very expensive, yet this is such an important part of the finished piece. You should always try to present your artwork in the best possible way. I economize by working in traditional sizes of mats and frames. When the project is heavily layered, use a double mat with a floater between the two layers.

1. Purchase the double mat and foam core board from an art store. Lay out the materials: tacky glue, masking tape, fleece, scissors, the finished project, and the inside mat. Set the outer mat aside.

2. Cut 2 pieces of fleece: one exactly the size of the inside opening of the mat, and one ¼˝ larger all around.

3. Turn the mat over and glue along the inside edge of the mat opening. Glue the art project into the mat. With tape, secure 2 sides, then pull the piece until taut; tape in place until all sides are secure. Set aside until completely dry.

4. Turn the mat over and lay the largest fleece directly behind the finished project.

5. Lay the smaller fleece behind the larger one, making sure it lines up with the actual mat opening. Smear tacky glue onto the back of the mat and lay the cardboard backing in place.

6. Turn the piece over, pressing firmly until the padding bulges. Lay a cloth over the mat (to protect it from smudges). Set heavy books atop the mat until it is completely dry.

7. Cut strips of foam core and glue along the front edges of the inside mat. Glue the outer mat to the strips. (Make sure the glass will not touch the artwork.) You may have to add more strips to make it deeper. Finally, take the piece to your art store for framing.

EMBROIDERY STITCHES

ALGERIAN EYE STITCH

1. Come up at A and go down at B (the center of the stitch) with a straight stitch. Come up at C.

2. Point B becomes the pivot point for the stitches.

3–6. Continue inserting the needle at point B to form the stitches along the designated line until finished. This stitch can have 8 or 16 long or short rays. For 16 rays, work a second set of straight stitches between each of the original 8. Use a second color for the last 8 stitches.

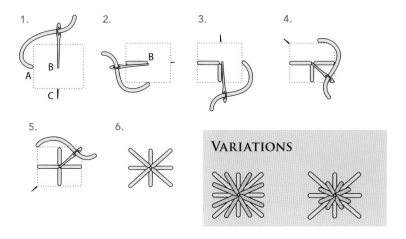

VARIATIONS

ARROWHEAD STITCH

Work the first row of slanted stitches from left to right.

1. Come up at A, pull through, and go down at B, emerging at C. Repeat for the rest of the row.

2–3. On the return pass, work the stitches in the same way, but from right to left, filling in the spaces. This keeps the stitches even. Use this stitch on its own or stack to make a filler stitch.

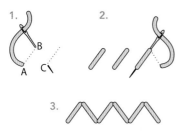

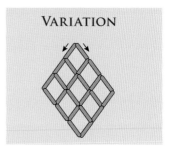

VARIATION

ARROWHEAD STITCH—STACKED

1. Come up at A, go down at B, then up at C.

2. Go down at B and up at D.

3. Continue until each arrowhead is completed, keeping the stitches evenly spaced.

ARROWHEAD LEAF

1. Mark the shape as a guide. Come up at A, go down at B, then up at C.

2–4. Continue working in this manner, keeping the stitches very close.

BACKSTITCH

Work individual stitches from right to left.

1. Come up at A, take a small backward stitch going down at B, and come up at C.

2–4. Always move the needle forward under the fabric and come up 1 stitch length ahead (D), ready to take another stitch.

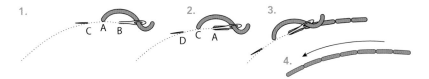

BACKSTITCH—THREADED

This stitch is composed of the backstitch (above) and 2 loop stitches worked with contrasting threads.

1. Come up at A, take a small backstitch to B, and come up at C.

2. Work the backstitches the length of the desired line. Come up at D with a contrasting thread. Slide the needle under the backstitches, alternating above and below the row without catching the fabric.

3–4. Interweave another contrasting thread to complete the loops.

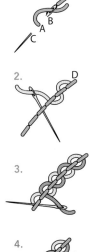

BASQUE KNOT

Work this stitch along 2 parallel lines.

1. Come up at A, go down at B, then up at C.

2. Slide the needle under the stitch between A and B, to the right of C (to the left of C if left-handed).

3. Loop the thread around the stitch again, bringing the needle tip over the thread.

4–5. Pull the thread to form a knot. Go down at D and come up at E to continue the next stitch.

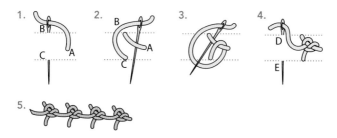

BRAID STITCH

1. Come up at A, go down at B, then up at C. Slide the needle under the straight stitch between A and B, go down again at D as close to C as possible but not into it, and come up at E.

2–3. Slide the needle under the straight stitch again. Go down at F and up at G.

4–5. Slide the needle under the chain stitches and continue with the next stitch.

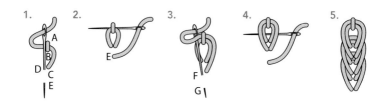

BULLION STITCH

Use double thread or silk buttonhole twist for a neater wrap.

1. Come up at A and go down at B, leaving a loop. Come up again at A with the needle tip only.

2. Raise the tip of the needle by holding it in your left hand and putting pressure on the top of the needle eye. Wrap the needle with the thread; pull the wrap firmly down toward the fabric.

3. Work the desired number of wraps until the wraps are the same width as the space from A to B. Pull the wraps firmly into place.

4. Hold the wraps and pull the needle through the wraps. Pull the thread through, holding firmly, pulling away from yourself in order to tighten the stitch. Go back into B to put the bullion stitch in place.

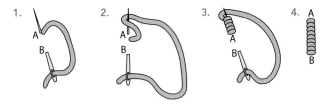

BULLION ROSE

1. For the rose center, work 3 bullion stitches (above) of equal length to form a triangle.

2–4. Work a bullion stitch to wrap around one corner of the triangle. Lengthen the stitches as needed so that each stitch curls around the others. Continue making bullion stitches around the triangle until the rose is complete.

BULLION ROSEBUD

1. Come up at A; pull the thread through. Go down at B. Come up again at A.

2. Wrap the needle several times to fill the desired length. Hold the wraps firmly and pull the needle through, away from yourself.

3. Pull the wraps toward yourself and anchor the bullion stitch by going back down at B.

4. If you are making 2 bullion stitches, work the stitches so they slightly curve toward each other.

5. For 3 bullion stitches, work the center bullion stitch first, then add the right and left bullion stitches so they curve toward the center.

6–8. For leaves and stem use a fly stitch. Come up at C, go down at D, and up at E. Pull the thread through and go down at F.

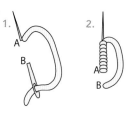
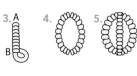

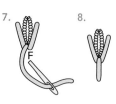

BUTTONHOLE STITCH

1. Come up at A, hold the thread down with your thumb, go down at B, and then up at C.

2–3. Bring the needle tip over the thread and pull into place. Repeat.

The horizontal thread should be on the seamline. Keep the vertical lines straight and even.

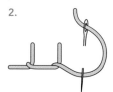
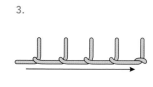

BUTTONHOLE STITCH—CIRCLE

This is a great stitch for hollyhocks, all saucer-shaped flowers, and underwater anemones.

1. Draw a circle the desired size of the flower. Bring the needle up at A (the outside of the circle). Go down at center B and come up at C, to the right of A (to the left of A if left-handed). Make sure the needle is over the thread; pull firmly.

2–4. Continue around the circle until it is filled.

BUTTONHOLE STITCH—CLOSED

This stitch is similar to the regular buttonhole, except that the tops of 2 vertical stitches tip toward each other and are worked into the same hole as B; this forms the triangle shape.

1. Come up at A, hold the thread down with your thumb, go down at B, and then up at C.

2. Bring the needle tip over the thread and pull into place. Go down at B and up at D to form the second side of the stitch.

3. Go down at E and up at F to begin the next stitch.

BUTTONHOLE STITCH—DETACHED

1. Draw an outline shape (example: leaf shape) on the fabric. Work a chain stitch (page 48) along the top of the outline. Work a row of buttonhole stitch (page 44) loops under the chain stitch. Keep the loops rather loose.

2. Once at the right end, take the thread back to the opposite end. Start another row of loops.

3. Continue to the desired width, filling in the designated shape.

BUTTONHOLE STITCH—KNOTTED

1. Come up at A and form a loop, wrapping the thread around your thumb. Slip the needle under the front of the loop.

2–3. Work the loop onto the needle. Insert the needle at B and come up at C; form a neat knot by gently tightening the loop before pulling the needle through the fabric.

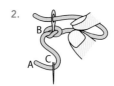

BUTTONHOLE STITCH—TRIANGLE

This is a wonderful stitch for floral shapes.

1. Draw a quarter-circle shape. Come up at A (at the outer left corner, or right corner if left-handed). Go back down at B, bringing the needle up close to A. Loop the thread under the needle and pull through.

VARIATION

2. Continue making stitches to fill in the area. End with a catch stitch.

Buttonhole Stitch—Up and Down

1. Come up at A and hold the thread down with your thumb. Go down at B and come up at C, bringing the needle tip over the thread.

2–4. Go down at D, then come up at E. Pull the thread to the top and then go down, inserting the needle under the loop. Now gently pull the thread until the loop is tightened. Repeat this process for a row of Up and Down Buttonhole stitches.

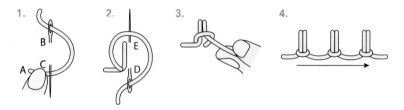

Cable Stitch

1. Come up at A, go down at B, then up at C (the center of the desired stitch length) keeping the working thread below the needle tip.

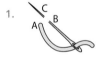

2–3. Work the next stitch in the same manner, keeping the thread above the needle tip. Stitch along the designated line, using small, even stitches and alternating the positions of the thread above or below the needle.

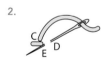

Cast-On Stitch Flower

1. Come up at A. Take a small backstitch toward A and leave the needle in the fabric.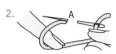

2. Grasp the thread in one hand and lay it over the index finger of your other hand (which is facing toward you).

3. Now twist your finger under the emerging thread so that the thread coming out of A lies on top.

4. Slip the loop onto the needle (cast on). Pull the thread tight and slip the loop down toward the fabric.

5. Continue to cast on more loops to make the desired length. Hold the stitches and pull the needle and thread through them.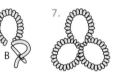

6-7. Go down at B and pull the thread through.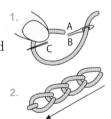

Chain Stitch

1-2. Come up at A and form a loop. Go down at B as close to A as possible, but not into it, and come up at C, bringing the needle tip over the thread. Repeat this stitch to make a chain.

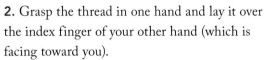
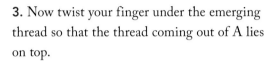

Chain Stitch—Cable

1. Come up at A and wrap the thread once around the needle.

2-3. Go down at B, then up at C, bringing the needle tip over the thread. Pull the thread taut after each stitch.

Chain Stitch—Detached Flower

1. Come up at A. Go down as close to A as possible but not into it, and come up at B. Make sure the needle lies over the loop; pull through.

2. Fill in the rest of the shape with the buttonhole stitch (page 44). End by taking the thread just over the last loop.

Chain Stitch—Detached Twisted

1. Come up at A and form a loop. Go down at B, even with and to the left of A (to the right of A if left-handed); then come up at C, bringing the needle tip over the thread.

2–3. Go down at D, making a small anchor stitch at the bottom of the loop.

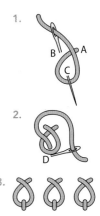

Chain Stitch—Magic

1. Thread the needle with 2 contrasting threads. Come up at A and form a loop. Go down at B as close to A as possible but not into it, and come up at C, looping only one thread under the needle tip. The first thread will appear as a single chain stitch, and the second will disappear behind the fabric.

2–3. Repeat, working the second thread under the needle tip. Continue stitching, alternating the first and second threads for the loops.

Chain Stitch—Open

Work this stitch along 2 parallel lines (think of a ladder with this stitch).

1. Come up at A and form a loop. Go down at B even with and to the right of A (to the left of A if left-handed); then come up at C, bringing the needle tip over the thread. Leave the loop loose.

2–3. Go down at D, over the loop, and come up at E for the next stitch. Anchor the stitch end with 2 catch stitches.

Chain Stitch—Rose

1. Mark a circle the size of the desired rose. Come up at A within the circle. Go down at B, then up at C, bringing the needle tip over the ribbon.

2–3. Repeat this stitch, making a continuous chain and working in a counterclockwise direction (clockwise if left-handed) to fill in the circle. This can be worked with thread, yarn, or silk ribbon.

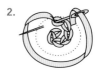

CHAIN STITCH—ROSETTE

Work this stitch along 2 parallel, horizontal lines.

1. Come up at A and form a loop. Go down at B, even with and to the left of A (to the right of A if left-handed), taking a small, slanting stitch; then come up at C, bringing the needle tip over the thread.

2. Pull the needle through and pass the needle tip under the top right thread at A.

3–4. Go down at D, then come up at E.

Use for flowers if worked in a circle or curve. Use as borders if worked in straight lines.

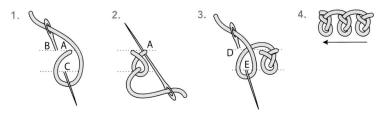

CHAIN STITCH—RUSSIAN

1. Come up at A and form a loop. Go down as close to A as possible but not into it, and come up at B, bringing the needle tip over the thread.

2. Go down at C, form a loop, and come up at D.

3. Go down at E to make an anchor stitch, then come up at F.

4–5. Repeat the steps to form the next looped stitch in the same manner.

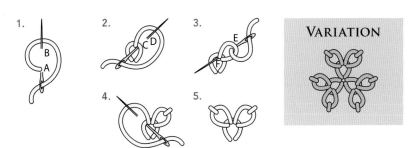

VARIATION

CHAIN STITCH—SPINY

This stitch is composed of the chain stitch (page 48) and straight stitch (page 86).

1. Come up at A and form a loop. Go down at B, then up at C, bringing the needle tip over the thread.

2. Go down at D, making a straight stitch the desired length, and come up at E.

3–4. Go down at F and come up at G, bringing the needle tip over the thread to continue the next stitch.

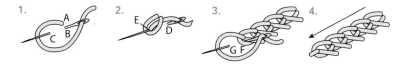

CHAIN STITCH—TWISTED

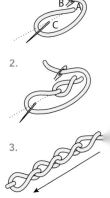

Work this stitch along a line.

1. Come up at A along the designated line and form a loop. Go down at B, slightly to the left of A (to the right of A if left-handed), and take a small, slanting stitch to C, bringing the needle tip over the thread.

2–3. Repeat this stitch for a continuous row.

CHAIN STITCH—WHIPPED

1. Make a row of continuous chain stitches (page 48).

2–3. Using a blunt needle to prevent snagging the chain stitches, thread up with a different thread or silk ribbon. Come up at point A and wrap the thread or silk ribbon around each individual chain stitch by bringing the needle under each stitch from the top. If using silk ribbon, keep it flat.

Judith Baker Montano's Essential Stitch Guide

Chain Stitch—Zigzag

1. Come up at A and form a loop. Go down at B, as close as possible but not into it, then up at C, bringing the needle tip over the thread.

2. Form another loop and go down at D, piercing the lower curve of the first loop to keep it in position, and come up at E. Continue, alternating the angle of the stitches.

3. End with a catch stitch.

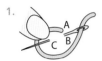

Chevron Stitch

Work this stitch from left to right along 2 horizontal parallel lines. Start on the bottom line.

1. Come up at A, go down at B, then up at C (in the center of the stitch).

2. Make an angled straight stitch the desired length to D, insert the needle, and come up at E.

3. Keep the thread loop on the top. Go down at F (equal to the length of A/B) and come up at G.

Continue working, alternating from one side to the other and keeping the stitches evenly spaced.

CHINESE KNOT

Also called a Peking Knot, this stitch is often found in antique Chinese embroidery. Use as a filler stitch and vary the colors of thread to achieve beautiful shading.

1. Come up at A and loop the thread.

2. Hold the loop down with your thumb and finger. Pick up the loop and flip it over so that the thread coming out of A is on the top.

3. Insert the needle inside the loop as close to A as possible but not into it.

4–5. Pull the knot firmly into place. Holding the thread taut with your thumb, push the needle through to the back.

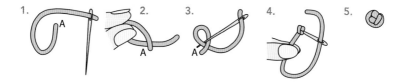

CHINESE KNOT—LOOPED

1–4. Work the Chinese Knot (above) up to the point of pulling the thread through to the back of the fabric.

5. Hold the loop at the desired length with your thumb. Pull the thread through to the back.

Tighten; the loop should sit on top of the knot.

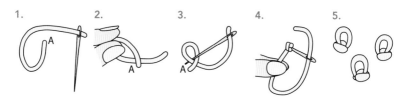

Colonial Knot

This knot sits up with a little dimple in the center.

1. Come up at A. Hold the thread loosely in your free hand and push it into a backward C.

2. Poke the tip of the needle into the backward C so that the thread lies on top of the needle. With your free hand, wrap the thread up, over, and under the tip of the needle. This forms a figure eight.

3. Pull the wraps firmly around the needle and go back into B, which should be right beside A.

4. Hold the knot firmly off to the side while you gently pull the thread through the fabric.

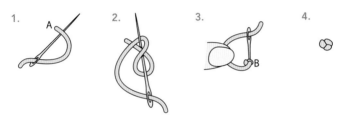

Coral Stitch

Work the stitch from right to left along a line.

1–3. Come up at A and lay the thread along the designated line. Bring the needle down at a right angle to the thread, go down at B and then up at C, bringing the needle tip over the thread.

Vary the knot by changing the length and angle of the vertical stitch.

CORAL STITCH—ZIGZAG

Work this stitch from right to left along 2 horizontal parallel lines.

1. On the top line come up at A, go down at B, then up at C, bringing the needle tip over the thread.

2. Reverse the loop on the lower line, moving it slightly to the left (to the right if left-handed). Go down at D and come up at E, bringing the needle tip over the thread.

3–4. Continue with the next stitch.

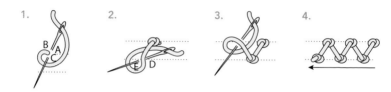

COUCHING STITCH

Couching is a decorative way to hold a long (placed) thread in place. Mark a line for the desired length of the laid thread.

1–2. Position the laid thread on the marked line. With either matching or contrasting thread or ribbon, come up at A and go down at B, wrapping a small stitch over the placed thread at regular intervals.

CRETAN STITCH

Work this stitch from left to right along 2 horizontal parallel lines.

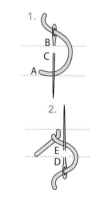

1. Come up at A. Go down at B and come up at C, taking a downward vertical stitch (the desired length), bringing the needle tip over the thread.

2–3. Go down at D, then up at E.

Be sure to keep the vertical stitches evenly spaced.

CRETAN STITCH—DECORATIVE

Work the stitch from top to bottom.

1. Mark the shape to guide the stitches. Come up at A, to the left of center (to the right if left-handed), go down at B, and then up at C, in the center of the stitch. Go down at D and come up at E, bringing the needle tip over the thread.

2–3. Continue stitching side to side until the shape is completely filled.

CROCHET CHAIN STITCH

This is a looped stitch formed with a crochet hook and resembles a chain stitch attached only at the fabric base. Great for organic shapes like tree trunks, seaweed, and shrubs.

1. Make a small straight stitch: come up at A, go down at B, and come up at A again.

2. Remove the needle from the thread. With a crochet hook, reach under the straight stitch and work up a series of crochet chain stitches. Work to the desired length. Rethread the needle and anchor the chain to the back. The chain stitch can be tacked down with another thread.

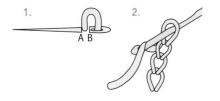

VARIATION

CROSS-STITCH

Work cross stitches from left to right.

1. Come up at A, go down at B, then up at C, making a row of even, slanted stitches.

2–3. On the return pass, cross over the first stitches to form Xs.

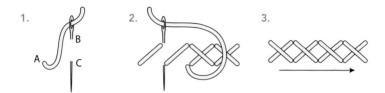

CROSS-STITCH—FLOWER

This is an interwoven diagonal cross-stitch.

1. Come up at A and go down at B. Cross over the stitch with an equal-sized stitch from C to D.

2. Come up again at A and cross over to B. Come up again at C to start the next stitch, weaving the thread through the stitches.

3–4. Continue weaving to make a larger decorative cross-stitch flower.

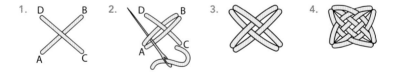

CROSS-STITCH—ST. GEORGE

1. Come up at A, go down at B, and then up at C, making a row of evenly spaced running stitches (page 81).

2–3. On the return pass, come up at D, go down at E, and come up at F, crossing each running stitch with a vertical stitch of equal length.

CROWN STITCH

This stitch is composed of a fly stitch (page 66) and 2 straight stitches (page 86).

1. Come up at A, go down at B, and come up at C, bringing the needle tip over the thread. Keep the stitch loose to form a slight curve.

2. Go down at D, then up at E, bringing the needle tip next to the working thread.

3. Go down at F and come up at G.

4–5. Insert the needle into H, to the left of the center straight stitch.

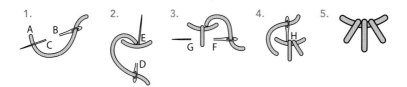

DOUBLE KNOT STITCH

Work this stitch from left to right along a designated line.

1. Come up at A, go down at B, and come up at C.

2–3. Slide the needle under the stitch and loop the thread around the stitch, bringing the needle tip over the threads.

4–5. Pull the thread to form the knot and continue with the next stitch.

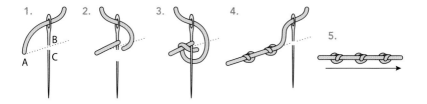

DRIZZLE STITCH

Use a straw needle for this very effective Brazilian stitch. Use for underwater seaweeds and flowers.

1. Come up at A. Unthread the needle and insert it next to A, using a pincushion or felt pad to hold the needle upright.

2. Place the thread over your index finger. Rotate your finger toward and then away from yourself, holding the thread taut.

3. Slip the loop off your finger onto the needle. Pull the thread tight; slip the loop down the needle to the fabric. This is the first cast-on stitch.

4. Work the desired number of cast-on stitches. Pull each stitch tightly and push it down onto the needle.

5. Rethread the needle. Pull the needle and thread through the cast-on stitches. This is the first petal, or drizzle. The stitches may be long or short.

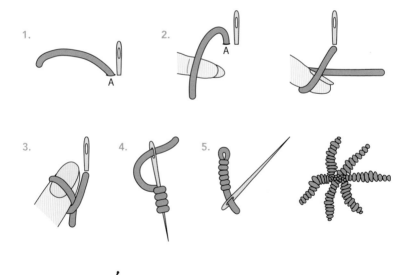

END-STRING FLOWERS

Save bits and pieces of thread and ribbon to make these tufted flowers.

1. Take various lengths of thread and tie them in a series of evenly spaced knots. Cut between the knots.

2. Hold the pieces by the knot and pull the ends up to form a loose pom-pom.

3. With a needle, separate any twisted threads to make the flowers even fluffier.

4. Sew the shape in place, taking the needle through the knot and wrapping once around the pom-pom threads; pull firmly in place.

Make plenty of these knotted flowers to keep for future projects.

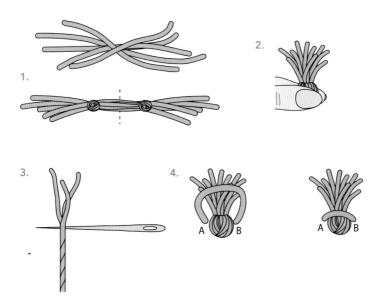

ERMINE STITCH

Work this stitch along 2 parallel lines.

1. Come up at A, go down at B, and come up at C.

2. Go down at D and come up at E.

3. Go down at F to complete the stitch.

This stitch can be scattered to form floral shapes and texture.

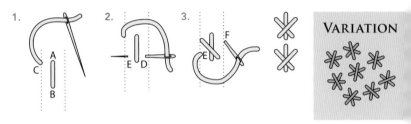

VARIATION

EYELET STITCH—FLOWER

1. Gently pierce a hole in the fabric with an awl. Make a small running stitch (page 81) just outside the hole. Take the needle through to the back.

2. Make a satin stitch (page 81) to cover the edge of the hole. Keep an even tension and continue around, covering the running stitch. Finish the satin stitch and take the thread through to the back. End by running the thread under the stitches to secure.

3. Work 4 straight stitches (page 86) on the sides or use 4 lazy daisy stitches (page 70).

EYELET—FREE FORM

1. Gently pierce a hole in the fabric with an awl. Come up at A, then go down into the center hole.

2. Come up again and work straight stitches around the center hole. Pull firmly to keep the hole open.

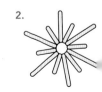

FEATHERSTITCH—SINGLE

1. Come up at A, go down at B, even with and to the left of A (to the right of A if left-handed), and come up at C.

2–3. Alternate the stitches back and forth, working them downward in a vertical column.

FEATHERSTITCH—DOUBLE

Work the double featherstitch in the same manner as the single featherstitch, but complete 2 stitches before alternating the direction. Stitches 1 and 3 are on the line; stitches 2 and 4 swing out.

FEATHERSTITCH—TRIPLE

Work the triple featherstitch in the same manner as the double featherstitch, but complete 3 stitches before alternating the direction. Stitches 1 and 4 are on the line; stitches 2, 3, 5, and 6 swing out.

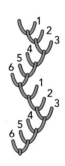

FEATHERSTITCH—CHAINED

Work this stitch along 2 parallel lines.

1. Come up at A and form a loop. Go down at B, as close to A as possible but not into it, and come up at C, bringing the needle tip over the thread.

2–3. Go down at D, making a slanted straight stitch the desired length. Come up at E and continue working the next stitch. Always work the straight stitches to form a regular zigzag pattern.

 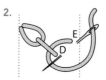 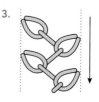

FEATHERSTITCH—CLOSED

Work this stitch along 2 parallel lines.

1. Come up at A, go down at B, then up at C, bringing the needle tip over the thread.

2–3. Go down at D and come up at E, bringing the needle tip over the thread.

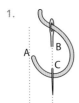
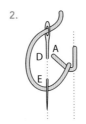
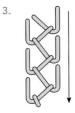

FEATHERSTITCH—LEAF

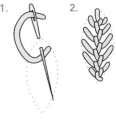

This is a free-form leaf that is easy to do because the stitches can be uneven.

1. Draw an outline of a leaf shape. Start at the top of the leaf with the featherstitch (page 63). Alternate the stitches left and right, working them downward in a vertical column.

2. Work out to the outside lines. These stitches are uneven and meant to be free form; they can also be worked in multiple layers of color.

VARIATION

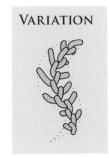

FERN LEAF STITCH

Mark a line the designated length of the fern leaf.

1. Come up at A and go down at B, making a straight stitch; come up again at A.

2. Go down at C, then come up again at A.

3–4. Go down at D, keeping the length of the stitches consistent with the first set. Come up at E and continue with the next stitch, forming the stitch along the marked line.

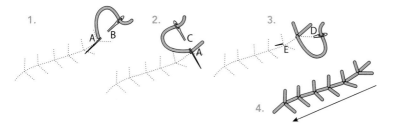

FISHBONE STITCH

Draw a leaf or other outline to guide the stitches.

1. Come up at A on the center line. Go down at B, then back up at C, keeping the thread on the right side of the needle (left side if left-handed).

2. Pull the thread through. With the thread on the left (on the right if you are left-handed), go down at D, then up at E.

3–4. Continue stitching to form the leaf.

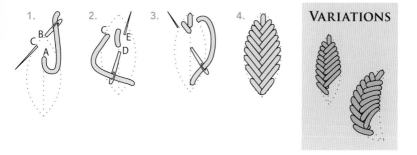

VARIATIONS

FISHBONE STITCH—OPEN

Draw a leaf outline to guide the stitches.

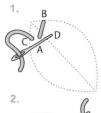

1. Come up at A and go down at B. Come up at C and go down at D, overlapping the stitch to cover the base of the first.

2. Work the stitches alternately over the center line to keep the spacing consistent. Continue working, alternating from side to side, until the shape is filled.

FLAT STITCH

Mark 2 lines down the center of the shape as a guide for the stitches.

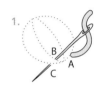

1. Come up at A, then go down at B; slip the needle tip under the fabric, and come up at C.

2–3. Continue working, alternating from side to side and keeping the stitches close together. Each new stitch will overlap the base of the previous stitch.

This stitch is wonderful for filling in leaves and petals.

FLY STITCH

1. Come up at A and go down at B, even with and to the right of A (to the left of A if left-handed); then come up at C, bringing the needle tip over the thread.

2–3. Draw the thread gently through the fabric. Go down at D, forming a catch stitch.

This stitch may be worked singly or stitched in rows.

VARIATION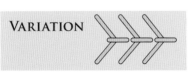

Fly Stitch—Circle

1. Come up at A and pull the thread through. Make a loop, go down at B, and come up at C, bringing the needle tip over the thread; pull into place.

2. Go down at D to finish.

3. Continue making stitches to form a circle.

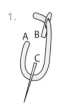

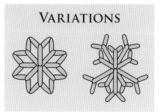

VARIATIONS

Fly Stitch—Dandelion Seed Pod

1. Work up a fly stitch (page 66) from A to C.

2. Hold the thread over to the left side (to the right if left-handed). Make a small lazy daisy stitch (page 70). Go down at D and up at E. Pull the stitch into place, making sure the needle lies over the thread. Anchor with a catch stitch at F.

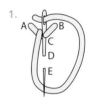

Fly Stitch—Leaf

Draw an outline of the leaf shape.

1. Come up at A, go down at B, up at C, and down at D.

2. Work a series of free-form fly stitches, going to the outside edges of the leaf. The center, or spine, of the leaf will be where the catch stitch (D) of the fly stitch is placed.

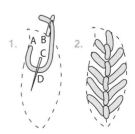

FRENCH KNOT

1. Come up at A and wrap the thread twice around the needle.

2–3. While holding the thread taut, go down at B, as close to A as possible but not into it. Hold the knot in place until the needle is completely through the fabric.

The French knot is good to use for flowers such as baby's breath and yarrow.

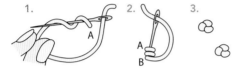

GRANITO

1. Come up at A and go down at B.

2. Come back up at A in the same hole. Pull the thread through. Loop the thread to the left and go back down at B (through the same hole); pull through and position the thread on the left.

3. Come back up at A and loop the thread to the right. Go back down at B.

Add extra stitches to make a larger granito stitch. The small bud-like shape may look different based on the number of stitches.

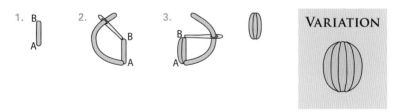

VARIATION

Head-of-the-Bull Stitch (Tête de Boeuf)

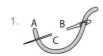

This stitch is composed of a fly stitch (page 66) and lazy daisy stitch (page 70).

1. Come up at A, go down at B, and come up at C, bringing the needle tip over the thread.

2. Go down at D, to the right of the working thread (to the left if left-handed), and come up at E, bringing the needle tip over the thread.

3–4. Take a small stitch at F to anchor the loop.

Herringbone Stitch

Work the stitch from left to right.

1. Come up at A, go down at B, and come up at C.

2–3. Continue working, alternating from top to bottom.

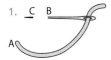
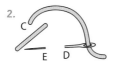

Herringbone Stitch—Laced

This stitch is composed of a modified herringbone (above) and a lacing thread.

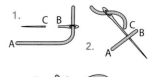

1. Come up at A, go down at B, and up at C.

2–3. Slide the needle under the slanted stitch. Go down at D, then up at E. Continue to make a row of stitches.

4–5. With a contrasting thread, come up at 1. Slide the thread under the first crossing of slanted stitches. Work it under the thread at 1, then over and under at the same crossing, bringing the thread to the lower crossing.

HOLBEIN STITCH

1. Come up at A and go down at B, making a straight stitch the desired length.

2. Continue, making a V shape of even, vertical stitches.

3–4. On the return pass, work the horizontal straight stitches in the same manner, filling in the spaces.

Use on borders or as a filler stitch.

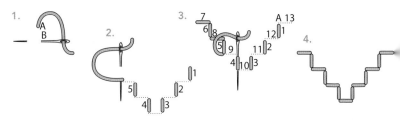

LAZY DAISY STITCH

This stitch is a free-floating chain stitch.

1. Come up at A and form a loop. Go down at B, as close to A as possible but not into it, and come up at C, bringing the needle tip over the thread.

2–3. Go down at D, making a small anchor stitch.

For effect, vary the length of the loop and the anchor stitch.

This stitch is good for petals and leaves.

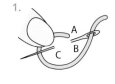

Lazy Daisy Stitch— with Bullion Stitch

1. Bring the thread up at A. Form a loop. Go back down at A and come out at B. Pull the loop snugly under the needle

2. Take the thread going into the needle and wrap the thread around the needle tip.

3. Make 4 or 5 wraps. Pull the wraps snugly.

4–5. Hold the wraps firmly with your thumb and pull the thread through the wraps. Pull the wraps tight. Anchor the stitch. Use the tip of the needle to push the wraps in place.

This stitch is good for shooting stars and leaves.

Lazy Daisy Stitch—Double

1. Come up at A and form a loop. Go back down at A and come up at B. Make sure the needle lies over the thread; pull through. Go down at C.

2–3. Come up just above A, forming a larger lazy daisy stitch on the outside.

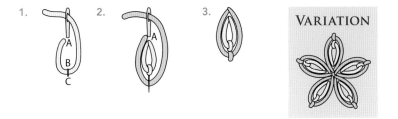

VARIATION

LEAF STITCH

Mark the shape to guide the stitches.

1. Come up at A, go down at B, and come up at C.

2–3. Work the stitches alternately on either center line to keep the spacing consistent. Continue in this manner, alternating from side to side, until the shape is filled. An outline of stem (page 84) or chain stitches (page 48) is usually worked around the leaf.

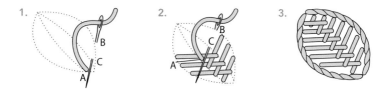

LONG AND SHORT STITCH

Mark the shape as a guide for the stitches.

1. Come up at A and go down at B, making a straight stitch the desired length; then come up at C.

2. Work the first row in alternating long and short satin stitches, keeping the outline of the shape even and defined.

3–4. Work the remaining satin stitch rows in equal lengths; vary the thread color to add shading. Use this stitch for shading or filling in large areas.

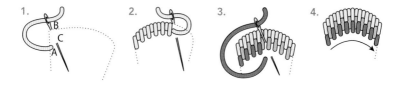

LOOP STITCH—THREAD

Work this stitch from right to left along 3 parallel lines.

1. Come up at A and go down at B. Come up at C, even with and directly below B, looping the thread under the first stitch and bringing the needle tip over the thread.

2–3. Continue working the next stitch, going down at D and coming up at E.

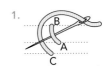

MAGIC CHAIN BAND STITCH

1. Come up at A and go down at B to make a line of straight stitches.

2. Thread the needle with 2 contrasting threads. Come up at C, loop only 1 thread under the needle, and insert the needle at D, as close to C as possible but not into it. Come up at E, bringing the needle tip over 1 of the threads as shown. That thread will appear as a single chain stitch, and the second thread will disappear behind the fabric.

3–4. Repeat the stitch, working the second thread under the needle. Continue stitching, alternating the first and second threads for the loops.

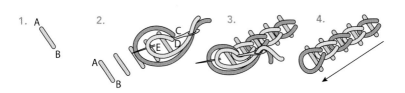

Maidenhair Stitch

This variation of the featherstitch has a fernlike quality.

1. Come up at A, go down at B, and come up at C, bringing the needle tip over the thread.

2–3. Work 3 single featherstitches (page 63) on one side, graduating the length of the stitches and aligning them vertically. Work a similar group on the opposite side.

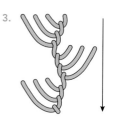

Needleweaving Bar

This stitch is used in needle lace but makes good leaves, petals, and sepals. Each bar is woven above the fabric with only the tip attached.

1. Come up at A. Form a loop and go down at B. Decide how wide the bar should be. Come up just below A at C.

2. Pass a paper clip through the loop to hold the loop off the fabric.

3. Weave *over* the bottom thread and *under* the top thread.

4. Come back *over* the top thread and *under* the bottom. After each pass, push the woven thread snugly down to the previous wraps.

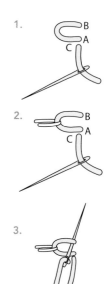

continued on page 75

Judith Baker Montano's Essential Stitch Guide

5. After the loop is wrapped, remove the paper clip.

6–7. Make the bar curve by going into the fabric at D, just a bit shorter than the length of the bar.

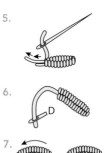

NET STITCH

This is a wonderful stitch for seaweed and fantasy leaves.

1. Make a row of stem stitches (page 84) to act as an anchor for the first row. Using a new thread, come up on the end of the stem stitch row at A. Holding down the thread, slide the needle under the first stem stitch, forming a loose buttonhole stitch (page 44). Make sure the needle lies over the loop.

2. Continue down the row.

3. Repeat this process for each row.

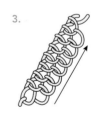

OPEN SQUARE STITCH

1. Come up at A and go down at B, making a straight stitch the desired length; then come up at C.

2. Make a backstitch at B and come up at D.

3–5. Continue in this manner, working in successive rows for borders or as a filler. For variety, change the thread colors in each row.

OVERCAST STITCH

Mark a line the designated length of the overcast stitch. Cut thread to this length and place it on the marked line.

1–3. Come up at A. Holding the cut threads on the marked line, go down at B and up at C, working small satin stitches with the wrapping thread. Keep the wraps close and even. When finished, take the ends of the cut threads to the back and secure.

This stitch is good for stems and outlines.

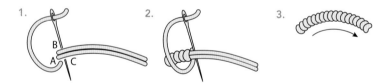

OYSTER STITCH

This stitch is a good stitch to use for texture and single petal shapes.

1. Come up at A and form a loop. Go down at B and come up at C with the needle over the thread. Pull the stitch into place.

2. Slide the needle under the thread, just below A.

continued on page 77

Judith Baker Montano's Essential Stitch Guide

3. Pull the thread through and allow the thread to lie on the right side of the twisted chain.

4. Go down inside the loop to the right of the twist (to the left if left-handed). Come up at the base with the needle over the loop.

5. Pull the thread through; the second loop lies around the first loop. Anchor the loop with a catch stitch.

PALESTRINA STITCH

Work this stitch from left to right along a designated line.

1. Come up at A, go down at B, and come up at C. Slide the needle under the stitch.

2. Loop the thread around the stitch again, bringing the needle tip *over* the thread.

3–4. Pull the thread to form a knot, go down at D, and come up at E to continue the next stitch. Space the knots evenly and close together to give a beaded look.

PALESTRINA STITCH—SQUARED

1. Come up at A, go down at B, and come up at C, keeping the stitches relatively loose. Slide the needle under the stitch, looping the thread around the stitch.

2–4. Loop the thread around the stitch again, bringing the needle tip over the thread. Pull the stitch snugly and go down at D. To make a continuous row, come up again at C (point A of the next stitch).

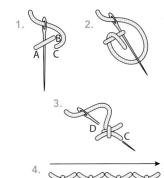

PEKINESE STITCH

This stitch is composed of backstitches (page 41) and a looping backstitch.

1. Come up at A, go down at B, and come up at C.

2–4. Make a line of backstitches to the length of the desired line. Using a thread of the same or a contrasting color, come up at 1, slide the needle under the previous backstitch, and loop the thread under the first backstitch, bringing the needle tip over the thread. Continue weaving the needle to complete the stitch.

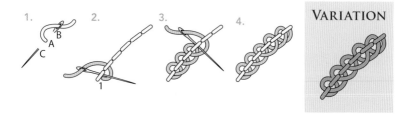

VARIATION

PETAL STITCH

This stitch is composed of a modified stem stitch (page 84) and a lazy daisy stitch (page 70).

1. Come up at A, go down at B, and come up at C (the midpoint of the previous stitch).

2. Form a loop and insert the needle at D, come up at E, and bring the needle tip over the thread.

3. Take a small stitch at F to anchor the loop and come up at G.

4. Insert the needle again at C and come up at B. Start the next stitch at B.

5. Continue to make a string of petal stitches.

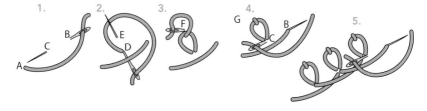

PISTIL STITCH

1. Come up at A, allowing a short length of thread, and wrap the working thread twice around the needle to form a French knot.

2–3. Go down at B (the length of the short thread plus the French knot), holding the knot in place until the needle is completely through the fabric.

This stitch is good for flower centers or free-form grass.

RAISED STRAIGHT STITCH

Mark the outer circle shape with dots. Mark a second, smaller circle in the center. Divide the circle into quarters as shown.

1. Come up on the center circle and go down on the outer circle.

2. Work each quarter circle with straight stitches.

3–4. Complete the circle. Fill the center with French knots (page 68). Raise the straight stitches by running the needle under the stitches and gently pulling them up.

RAMBLER ROSE

1. Work a small cluster of French knots (page 68) for the center. Come up at A, go down at B, and come up at C.

2. Do 2 or 3 rounds of loose stem stitches (page 84) around the knots. Make the stem stitch longer with each round.

ROMANIAN COUCHING STITCH

1. Come up at A. Carry across the space to be filled. Go down at B and come up at C.

2. Bring the thread up and over the laid thread. Go down at D and come up at E. This will create a diagonal couching stitch.

3–4. Continue down the laid thread at equal intervals.

ROSETTE STITCH

1. Come up at A and make a loop, go down at B, and come up at C, leaving the needle in the fabric.

2. Pull the working thread up and carefully wrap it around the needle 3 or 4 times. Try to keep the threads flat and side by side.

3–4. Pull the needle through slowly and go down at D, tacking the rosette at both ends.

RUNNING STITCH

Work the stitch from right to left.

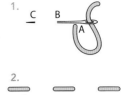

1–2. Come up at A, go down at B, and come up at C. Continue making small, even stitches that are the same length as the spaces between them.

RUNNING STITCH— LACED OR WHIPPED

This stitch is composed of a running stitch (above) and a whipstitch or lacing thread. Work the stitch from right to left.

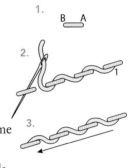

1. Come up at A and go down at B, working the running stitch the desired length.

2–3. For a whipped stitch, use a thread of the same or contrasting color and come up at 1, sliding the needle under the running stitches at even intervals.

VARIATION

For a laced stitch, use a contrasting thread and come up at 1, sliding the needle under the running stitches while working above and below them.

SATIN STITCH

Mark the shape as a guide for the stitches.

Work this stitch in single or double layers to create a thick, smooth blanket of stitching. The stitch can be worked straight up and down, side to side, or at an angle by laying straight stitches close together to conform to an outlined shape.

1. Come up at A and down at B. Emerge at C.

2. Continue this sequence to fill in the shape.

SCROLL STITCH

Work this stitch from left to right.

1–3. Come up at A. Loop the working thread to the right (to the left if left-handed) and hold it in place with your thumb. Go down at B and come up at C, making a small slanted stitch in the center of the loop. Tighten the loop around the needle and pull the needle through. Continue to make a line of stitches.

SEED STITCH

1–2. Come up at A and go down at B, making a small backstitch the desired length. Repeat for a second stitch, working the thread in the same holes, side by side.

VARIATION

Surround the seed stitches with an outline of backstitches if using for leaves.

SHEAF STITCH

1. Come up at A and go down at B, making a straight stitch the desired length. Work 2 more straight stitches of equal length, evenly spaced with the first.

2. Come up at the center of the straight stitch series and loop the thread around the stitches.

3. Pull the loop taut and go back down at the center, forming a catch stitch. For variety, change the length of the straight stitches, the number of loops, or move the catch stitch to the top or bottom of the row of straight stitches.

SNAIL TRAIL STITCH

Work this stitch from right to left along a designated line.

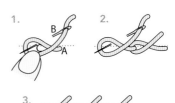

1–3. Come up at A, make a loop, and hold the thread with your thumb. Go down at B and come up at C, bringing the needle tip over the thread. Vary the stitch by altering the spacing and the slant of the stitch.

SPIDER WEB—BACKSTITCH

1. Use a tapestry needle and stitch the spokes as shown (up at A, down at B, up at C, down at D, and so on), pulling each spoke firmly in place.

2. Make a small stitch in the center, holding down all the spokes.

3. Come up to the top in the center. Slide under 1 spoke.

4. Continue working, easing back over 1 spoke and advancing under 2 stitches. Continue until the spokes are filled; wrap the thread back around the spoke.

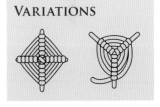

VARIATIONS

SPLIT STITCH

Use a heavier thread for this stitch or the thread will be difficult to split.

1–2. Come up at A, make a small backstitch to B, and then come up at C, piercing the working thread in the middle.

STAR STITCH

This star design is made of multiple straight stitches (page 86).

1. Come up at A and go down at B (point B becomes the center pivot of the stitch). Continue stitching 6 or 8 spokes, keeping them of equal length and spaced evenly.

2–3. Connect the spokes with straight stitches on the edges.

STAR FILLING STITCH

1. Come up at A and go down at B, making a straight stitch the desired length. Come up at C, go down at D, and come up at E, crossing the stitch with an equally sized horizontal stitch.

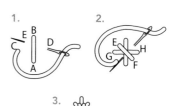

2–3. Work slightly smaller, equal-sized diagonal stitches: E to F and G to H. Finish with a tiny center cross.

STEM STITCH

Note: For a straight line of stem stitches, the thread length will always be above the line (away from you). For a curved line of stem stitches, the thread length will be outside the curved line and the needle will always come up inside the curve (C).

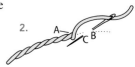

1–3. Come up at A and go down at B with a short, slanting stitch. Come up at C (the midpoint of A and B). Repeat, keeping the stitches small and uniform.

Stem Stitch—Portuguese

1. Come up at A, go down at B, and come up at C (the midpoint of the A/B stitch).

2–3. Pull the thread through and slide the needle under the stitch. Repeat, making 2 loops around the stitch.

4–6. Continue with the next stitch, always working beside the previous stitch.

Stem Stitch—Whipped

Note: For a straight line of stem stitches, the thread length will always be above the line (away from you). For a curved line of stem stitches, the thread length will be outside the curved line and the needle will always come up inside the curve (C).

This stitch is composed of a stem stitch (page 84) and a whipstitch.

1–2. Come up at A and go down at B with a short, slanting stitch. Come up at C (the midpoint of A and B). Repeat, keeping the stitches small and uniform.

3–4. Using matching or contrasting thread, come up at 1 and slide the needle under the stem stitches, working the whipstitches at even intervals without catching the fabric.

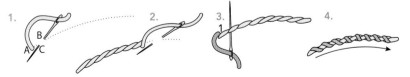

STRAIGHT STITCH

1–2. Come up at A and go down at B, making the stitch the desired length. Pull the thread firmly in place.

Straight stitches can be worked evenly or irregularly. They can vary in length and direction, but do not make the stitches too loose or too long or they could snag.

STRING OF PEARLS STITCH

1. Come up at A. Hold the thread in a horizontal line with the left hand (right hand if left-handed). Hold the needle perpendicular to the thread. With the tip of the needle over the thread, take a small stitch down at B, then come up at C. Pull firmly into place.

2. Take the thread up under the stitch to the right of the knot. Place the thread in a small circle surrounding the knot.

3–4. Go down just below the stitch at D, close to the knot. Come up next to the knot at E; pull taut. Continue stitching to make knots to the desired length.

SWORD EDGE STITCH

1. Come up at A, go down at B, and come up at C, leaving the stitch fairly loose.

2. Slide the needle under the stitch.

3. Go down at D and come up at E (point A of the next stitch).

4. Continue in the same manner to make a row of stitches.

Tufted Flower Stitch

This is a very free-form stitch to use for thistle and fuzzy-looking flowers.

1. Thread a needle with 3 or 4 strands of thread. Do not pull the thread into a knot. Go down at A and come up B, as close as possible but not into A. Decide how long the tufts will be.

2. With sharp scissors, clip the threads to the desired length.

3. The tufts will stay in place. Work the tufts close together to fill in the desired area.

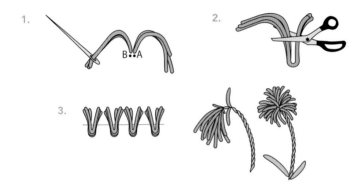

Tulip Stitch

This stitch is composed of a chain stitch (page 48) and a straight stitch (page 86).

1. Come up at A and form a loop. Go down at B, then come up at C, bringing the needle tip over the thread.

2. Take a small stitch at D to anchor the bottom of the loop, then come up at E.

3–5. Slide the needle under the anchor stitch and go down at F.

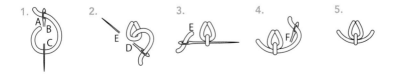

Turkey Work Stitch

Work from the top of the fabric.

1. Go down at A and leave a ½″ tail. Holding the tail under your thumb, come up at B, and go down again at A.

2–3. Come up again at B and trim the second thread tail to match the first. To make a continuous row of uncut stitches, slide a pencil under each loop while stitching to keep the loops uniform.

Use for looped flowers; cut the loops to achieve a furry look.

 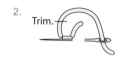 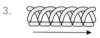

Van Dyke Stitch

Work this stitch between 2 parallel lines.

1. Come up at A, go down at B, and come up at C. Go down at D and come up at E.

2–3. Slide the needle under the crossed threads and gently pull the loop into place. The V formed at the top of the stitch should flare. Avoid pulling too tight or the center will be misshapen.

Wheat Ear Stitch

Mark a line the desired length of the stitch.

1. Come up at A and go down at B, making a slanted stitch, then come up at C, even with and to the right of A (to the left of A if left-handed). Go down again at D, as close to B as possible but not into it, and come up at E.

2. Slide the needle under the slanted stitches to form a loop.

continued on page 89

Judith Baker Montano's Essential Stitch Guide

3–4. Go down again at F, as close to E as possible but not into it, and come up at G, bringing the thread over the needle. Continue with the next stitch.

WHEAT EAR STITCH— DETACHED

1. Come up at A, go down at B, and come up at C. Keep the needle over the looped thread. Pull down and hold the thread with your free hand.

2–3. Make a second loop. Go down at C and up at D. Anchor with a small stitch.

WOOL ROSE

Use wool thread or tapestry yarn for this easy, effective rose.

1. Come up at A and go down at B. Bring the needle up a few threads above A. Pull the thread through to make the first stitch. Make a total of 5 stitches, making a square center.

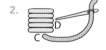

2. With a lighter shade of thread, come up at C and go down at D. Make a total of 3 stitches.

3. Come up at E (overlapping D) and go down at F. Make a total of 3 stitches.

4. Come up at G (overlapping F) and go down at H. Make a total of 3 stitches.

5–6. Bring the thread up at I (overlapping H) and go down at J (overlapping C). Make a total of 3 stitches.

WOOL ROSEBUD

1. Come up at A and go down at B.

2. Alternating from side to side, make 4 more flat stitches.

3. With another color of thread, come up left of the base center and take the thread up about ⅔ to the right side. Make 2 more stitches to complete the first petal.

4. With a third shade of thread, come up to the right of the base, overlapping the first petal. Take the thread up ⅔ of the bud. Make 3 stitches to complete the bud.

5. Change to green thread for the sepal. Make 2 short straight stitches (page 86) at the base. Make the stem using a stem stitch (page 84) or a stem stitch—whipped (page 85).

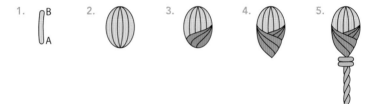

WOVEN PICOT

Use for a leaf or a petal.

1. Using a tapestry needle, work a pyramid of 3 straight stitches (page 86) the desired length of the petal. Make a secure knot at the back to secure the anchor stitches.

2–3. Come up at F. Weave under and over the stitches until you come to the tip. Go to the back and make a secure knot.

VARIATION

SILK RIBBON STITCHES

BRADFORD ROSE

1. Form the rose center with a French knot (page 68) or colonial knot (page 55).

2. Working around the knot, stitch 3 curved whipstitches (page 111).

3–4. Work 4 or 5 more curved whipstitches in a circle around the previous round. For variety, use dark ribbon in the center, fading to light ribbon around the edges.

1.

2.

3.

4.

COUCHED ROSE

This rose works best with 4mm- or 7mm-wide ribbon. Use 2 threaded needles for variety, threading one with a dark and one with a light shade of ribbon.

1. Come up at A and form a U shape. Go down at B, keeping the ribbon loose. Couch the U (page 56).

2–3. Continue working around the center U, couching the ribbon to form the rose.

Decorative Lazy Daisy Stitch

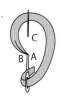

This is a simple lazy daisy stitch with a straight stitch added.

1. Come up at A and form a loop. Go down at B, then come up at C, keeping the ribbon flat and bringing the needle tip over the ribbon.

2–3. Go down at D, forming a small anchor stitch at the top of the loop. With another color ribbon, come up again at A and go down just below C.

This stitch is good for flower buds, sweet peas, and lupines.

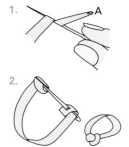

French Knot Flower

This small, loose, loopy stitch can be used separately or clustered.

1. Use a short length of ribbon (12″). Come up at A. Make 1 full wrap on the needle.

2. Go back into the fabric as close to A as possible but not into it. Do not pull the knot tight. Pull the needle and ribbon gently to the back. Leave a very loose French knot on the fabric.

3. With thread, come up in the center of the ribbon knot and make a French knot to anchor the ribbon and form the center of the flower.

French Knot Loop Stitch

1. Come up at A, make a loop, and hold it in place with a straight pin. Form a French knot (page 68) center by wrapping the ribbon twice around the needle. Go down at B (close to the pin).

continued on page 93

2. Gently pull the knot into place. Keep the ribbon taut while pulling the needle through to the back. For variety, stitch a colonial knot center (page 55).

Gathered Ribbon Flower

Make with silk or organza ribbon. The size of the flower is determined by the width and length of the ribbon.

1. Cut a 15″ length of 7mm silk ribbon. Using matching-colored thread, sew a line of small running stitches (page 81) along the edge of the ribbon.

2. Evenly gather the running stitches until the ribbon is half its original length. Fold the end down and secure with a knot.

3. Draw the shape of the flower onto the fabric. Anchor the ribbon to the center of the flower shape using 2 small stitches.

4–5. Fold the ribbon around the center. Stitch it in place every ⅛″ or so. Continue around in a spiral, until the shape is filled. End by turning the ribbon edge under and attaching it with 2 small stitches. Go to the back and make a knot.

HELEN'S ANTIQUE ROSE

Helen Eriksson is a household name in Australia. She uses two shades of 7mm or 4mm silk ribbon and a simple Japanese ribbon stitch (page 96) for this rose.

1. For the base petals, start from the center using the darkest shade. The petals will curve upward.

2. Add the shadow petals using a lighter shade.

3. Add 4 outer bowl petals, keeping them loose. Add a few more petals inside the outer bowl petals.

4. Work French knots (page 68) to fill in the center. Add 3 or 4 shorter petals in the center front.

IRIS STITCH

1. Form a loose lazy daisy stitch (page 70): Come up at A, then form a loop stitch (page 101), going back down at A and up at B. Pull the loop gently into place. Go down at C to anchor the loop.

2. Come up at D and slide the ribbon under the base of the lazy daisy stitch (try to keep it smooth). Go down at E.

3. Make a colonial knot (page 55) at the base of the lazy daisy stitch. Add a stem using stem stitches and long Japanese ribbon stitches for leaves.

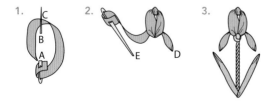

IVA'S ROSE

Iva Galloway from Puyallup, Washington, is the creator of this wonderful rose. Use about 12″ of either 7mm or 4mm silk ribbon.

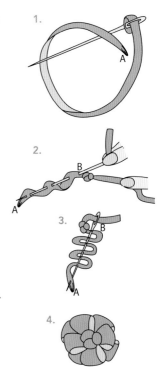

1. Come up at A and measure 2½″ to 3″ of 7mm ribbon or 1½″ to 2″ of 4mm ribbon. Tie a firm slipknot.

2. Insert the needle at B, just below the knot. Make zigzagging running stitches on 7mm ribbon and straight running stitches on 4mm ribbon.

3. Go down into A, avoiding the knot!

4. Pull gently into place. The slipknot acts as a stopper and forms the center of the rose.

JAN'S ANTIQUE ROSE

This beautiful rose was created by Jan Bond of Adelaide, Australia.

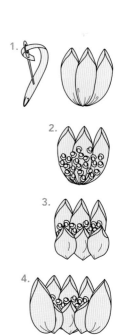

Use 4mm ribbon for small roses or 7mm ribbon for medium roses.

1. Stitch 3 Japanese ribbon stitches (page 96) close together.

2. Fill in with French knots (page 68). These will show toward the top and will act as padding for the overlapping stitches.

3. Add 3 Japanese ribbon stitches in front, keeping them very loose.

4. Add 2 longer Japanese ribbon stitches on either side.

Japanese Ribbon Stitch

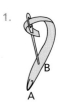

1. Come up at A, make sure the ribbon lies flat on the fabric, and pierce the center of the ribbon at B.

2. Gently pull the needle through to the back. The ribbon edges will curl at the tip. (The whole effect will be lost if the ribbon is pulled too tightly.)

Vary the petals and leaves by adjusting the length and tension of the ribbon before piercing with the needle. Use for bluebells, asters, lily, and iris leaves.

VARIATION

Joyce's Fargo Flower

This version of Ruth's Ruched Ribbon (page 106) was created by Joyce Valley of Fargo, North Dakota.

1. Use about 12″ of 4mm-wide silk ribbon and a chenille needle. Come up at A and hold the ribbon in your free hand.

2. With the tip of the needle held very close to point A, take 3–5 long running stitches through the ribbon.

3. Gently pull the needle to gather the ribbon.

4–5. Go back down as close to point A as possible but not into it. Pull the ribbon through and pull gently into place.

Judith's Curled Leaf

This can be worked in 4mm, 7mm, and 12mm silk ribbon. This is a variation on the Japanese ribbon stitch (page 96).

1. Come up at A. Slide the needle under the ribbon to smooth it out. Decide on the length of the stitch; with the tip of the needle at B, push the ribbon (in the center) into a curl or curve.

2. Pierce through to the fabric below and gently pull the ribbon through. Use your finger or a laying tool to keep it smooth and even. Do not let the ribbon twist.

3–4. Pull until a small roll appears at the tip of the leaf. Be careful not to pull too tightly or the leaf will become a short Japanese stitch.

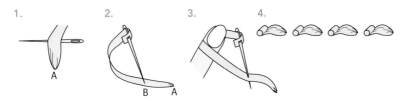

Judith's Knotted Flowers

Draw the outline of the flower on the fabric using a water-erasable pen. Use 4mm silk ribbon (about 12″) in 3 different shades, and a chenille needle.

1. Come up at A with the ribbon.

2. Make a knot at the desired height (¼″ to ½″). With the needle tip, work the knot into place and tighten. Go down at A.

3. Come up again near A, and use the needle as a laying tool to make sure both sides of the knot are even. Repeat the process until the area is filled.

Lazy Daisy Stitch—Rose

1. Come up at A and go down at B to make a Japanese ribbon stitch (page 96).

2. Come up at A and make a lazy daisy stitch (page 70).

3. Come up at A again and make a larger lazy daisy stitch on the other side.

4. Make straight stitches (page 86) at the bottom center.

Lazy Daisy Stitch—Rosebud

1. Come up at A and form a loop. Go back down at A and up at B. Gently pull the ribbon through point B.

2. Pierce the ribbon at the top of the loop. Pull into place to secure the stitch, letting this catch stitch remain a bit loose.

3–4. With thread or yarn, make a fly stitch (page 66) and a colonial knot (page 55) at the base to form the calyx.

Variation

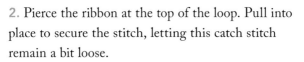

Lazy Daisy Stitch—with Bullion Tip

1. Come up at A and form a loop. Go down at B, as close to A as possible but not into it, and come up at C, bringing the needle tip over the ribbon. Keep the ribbon flat and wrap the ribbon around the needle 2 or 3 times.

2. Hold the twists in place with your thumb and pull the needle through.

continued on page 99

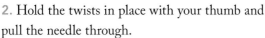

3. Hold the twists firmly on the fabric and go down at D making a bullion stitch and anchoring the stitch to the fabric.

LAZY DAISY STITCH—WITH FRENCH KNOT

1. Using a 4mm ribbon, come up at A. Make a loop, go back down in A, and come up at B. Pull the ribbon loop under the needle tip at B.

2. Extend the needle tip—but not the eye—over and beyond the loop. Raise the needle tip by applying pressure to the eye of the needle. Wrap the ribbon twice around the needle. Holding the wraps, firmly pull through the needle and the ribbon.

3–4. Catch the ribbon loop with the needle as you go back down, as close to B as possible.

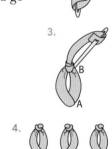

VARIATION

LEAF RIBBON STITCH

Mark a vertical line the desired length of the leaf.

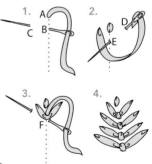

1. Come up at A and go down at B, forming a straight stitch; then come up at C.

2–4. Go down at D, to the right and even with C (to the left and even with C if left-handed), and come up at E, bringing the needle tip over the ribbon. Go down at F, forming a small anchor stitch. Continue with the next stitches, flaring out wider and wider to form a leaf.

LOOP FLOWER

1. Mark a small circle as a guide for the stitches and draw the points of each petal (3, 4, or 5).

2. Come up at A (the center of the circle) and go down ⅛″ away at B. Over a round toothpick, adjust the loop to be as long as the radius of the circle. Keep the toothpick in place until you complete the next loop to avoid pulling the previous petal out of shape.

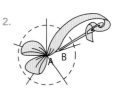

3–4. After completing the petals, thread an embroidery needle with floss and add French knots (page 68) or pistil stitches (page 79) to the flower centers to anchor the loops.

For the larger flowers, use 7mm ribbon and a large-eyed needle.

This stitch is good for thistledown (3 petals), California poppy and evening primrose (4 petals), and pansies and briar rose (5 petals).

LOOP FLOWER—BUD

1–2. Come up at A and go down at B. Gently pull the ribbon to form a loop. Do not let the ribbon twist. Use your finger or a laying tool to keep the loop straight. Pull the loop to the desired size.

3–4. Thread a needle with the desired thread. Flatten the ribbon loop in the center so that the loops are even. Bring the thread up through the center of the loop. Make a French knot (page 68) to anchor. Pull the thread tightly so the 2 sides of the ribbon form a bow.

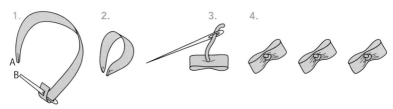

Loop Stitch—Ribbon

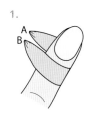

1–2. Using 4mm silk ribbon, come up at A and go back down at B. Use your finger or a laying tool to prevent the loop from twisting. Gently pull it to the desired length.

Work the loops close together. (Please use caution, as this stitch can be pulled out if you pull too hard.)

Montano Knot

1–2. Come up at A and wrap the ribbon around the needle (use 1–6 wraps, depending on the desired size); keep the wraps loose. Insert the needle back into the fabric at B, as close to A as possible but not into it. Pull through, but do not hold the ribbon off to one side as with other knots. Avoid pulling the stitch tight; let the knot be loose and flowery.

These glorified French knots are wonderful as fillers and floral sprays.

Variation—Cascade

Choose three different variegated 4mm ribbons or three shades of a color. Use 16″ lengths of ribbon and a chenille needle.

Choose a ribbon and begin making a row of Montano knots, decreasing from 7 wraps to 1 wrap, and form a slight curve with them.

Come back with the second ribbon and fill in around the previous stitches, again going from 7 wraps to 1 wrap.

Repeat the process with the third ribbon.

Fill in with green loops and Judith's Curled Leaf (page 97).

PANSY STITCH

Select 4 shades of 4mm silk ribbon, one being the base shade, such as purple. It can also be worked in wider ribbon.

1–2. Mark the center of the pansy with a dot on the fabric. Add 5 additional dots, as shown. Thread a chenille needle with the base shade and 1 of the 3 shades. Treat it as 1 ribbon. The first (or base) shade goes on top. Come up at the center mark and make a loose loop. Make a stitch to secure the loop, making a lazy daisy stitch (page 70).

3. Make a second lazy daisy stitch (2). Using the base shade and the second shade, make the next petal (3); the second shade goes on top.

4. Using the base shade and the third shade, make the remaining petals (4 and 5). The third shade goes on top. Make a colonial knot (page 55) in the center. Using a dark thread, make a straight stitch in the center of the 3 bottom petals.

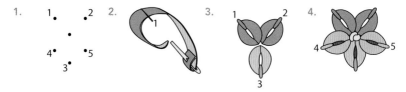

PLUME STITCH

Work the stitch from top to bottom.

1. Come up at A and go down ⅛″ away at B to make a loop; control it with a round toothpick.

2–3. Hold the loop in place and come up at C, piercing the fabric and the previous ribbon loop. Form another loop. Continue working downward until the plume is finished.

Raised Ribbon Stitch

Use 4mm up to 12mm silk ribbon.

Draw a circle that will be the actual size of the flower. Draw a dot in the center.

1. Come up with the ribbon just above the center dot. Use the needle to flatten the ribbon.

2. Gently raise the ribbon to form a curve, and pierce the center of the ribbon at the drawn-circle line.

3. Carefully pull the ribbon through, until the end starts to curl and pops through. Come up directly below the dot and make the second petal.

4. Add petals 3 and 4 to make a cross. Add petals 5, 6, 7, and 8 to make a full flower.

5. Add French knots (page 68) to the center.

Ribbon Split Stitch

The split stitch is worked the same way if using ribbon or thread.

1. Come up at A and go down at B. Use the needle to keep the ribbon flat.

2. Come up in the center of the straight stitch at C, flatten the ribbon with the needle, and go back down at D.

3. Continue stitching for the desired length.

tip

If worked with fine thread, this stitch is known as the Kensington outline stitch and can be used to outline or to act as a filler. Shading can be achieved with this stitch if it is worked in rows.

Ribbon Stitch Pansy

1. Mark dots as shown.

2. Come up just beyond the center mark. Slide the needle under the ribbon to flatten it and gently lift it up. Pierce the ribbon in the center at the marked dot (1). Pull the ribbon through until it curls, making a Japanese ribbon stitch (page 96).

3. Work the next petal (2) until it is snug against the first. Change the color of ribbon and work the bottom petal (3) in the same way.

4–5. Using a third shade of ribbon, make the final 2 stitches. Fill the center with a loose colonial knot (page 55). Using a dark thread, make 3 straight stitches on each of the 3 bottom petals.

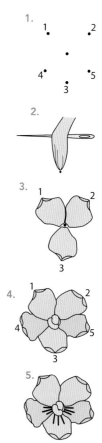

Rosette Bud

1–2. While keeping the ribbon flat, come up at A and go down at B, making a small straight stitch. Come up at C and go down at D, creating a padded straight stitch; do not pull the ribbon tight.

3–4. Angle the second padded stitch to one side, covering the base of the first. Angle the third padded stitch to the other side, covering the base of the second.

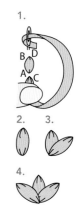

RUTH'S ROSETTES

Ruth Stonely of Brisbane, Australia, was a wonderful designer and a dear friend. This continuous line of rosettes can meander or form geometric patterns.

Make sure the running stitches are large and uneven.

1. Take a length of 4mm silk ribbon. Using a metallic, smooth thread on a fine needle, anchor stitch an end of the ribbon firmly into the edge of the fabric. On the back of the fabric, come up ¼″ beyond the anchor stitches. Keep a space between each rosette, usually ¼″ to ⅛″. Hold the ribbon.

2–4. Take 4 running stitches (page 81), so that 4 "bumps" are on the needle. End the needle under the ribbon. Pull the needle and thread through and go back down at point A to gather the ribbon into a small flower.

5–6. Make a knot on the back side to hold the flower in place. Hold the remaining ribbon flat and come up in the middle, ¼″ away from the flower. Repeat to make the next flower.

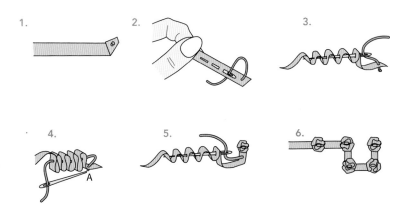

RUTH'S RUCHED RIBBON

Ruth Stonely taught me this technique. Use a long length of 4mm silk ribbon.

1. Thread a fine needle with smooth metallic thread. Anchor the ribbon firmly to the fabric with the thread by making a knot on the backside of the fabric.

2. Bring the needle back up. Hold the ribbon in your free hand and take large, uneven running stitches in the middle of the ribbon (the sloppier the stitches, the better the ruching looks!).

3. After 3″ to 4″ of running stitches, go into the fabric at B.

4. Pull gently and the ribbon will gather up between A and B.

5. Come back up in the center of the ribbon and make 3″ to 4″ of running stitches. End under the ribbon and sew it ½″ from point B. Use the needle tip to arrange the gathers. The gathers can be very loose or tight, depending on the distance taken and the number of gathers.

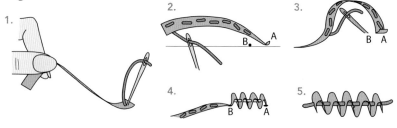

VARIATION

For a fuller look and more contrast, use two 4mm silk ribbons laid side by side. A second ribbon can be added into a single line of ruched ribbon. Anchor the second ribbon into the desired area and hold the 2 ribbons in your free hand. Make sure the ribbons overlap just slightly on the inside edges. Now take large, uneven running stitches along those overlapping edges. Let the ribbons overlap and change sides.

SIDE RIBBON STITCH

Unlike the Japanese ribbon stitch, the ribbon is pierced on a side instead of the center.

1. Come up at A, using 4mm silk ribbon (or wider). Slip the needle under the ribbon while holding the ribbon in place. Slide the needle down under the ribbon to flatten it.

2. Pierce the ribbon on the left side to make the right side curl in.

3. Pierce the ribbon on the right side to make the left side curl in.

4. Continue making stitches to create a flower.

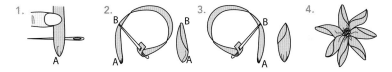

SPIDER WEB ROSE

Draw a circle on the fabric.

1. Use green thread for the spokes. Come up at A, go down at B even with and to the right of A (to the left of A if left-handed), and then come up at C, bringing the needle tip over the thread.

2. Gently draw the thread through the fabric. Go down at D, forming a catch stitch.

3. Add a stitch of equal length on each side, forming 5 spokes. Come up in the center of the spokes with the thread.

4–5. Use a short length of ribbon, about 8″–10″. Come up at the center and weave the ribbon over and under the spokes. After weaving around twice, pull the ribbon to form a firm center. Now twist the needle to add some twists to the ribbon. This creates lovely, full petals and fills in faster. Weave the ribbon until all the spokes are covered. Bring the ribbon to the back and tie off.

STAB STITCH

This is a single, spaced stitch worked in a regular or irregular pattern. The stitch width can vary, but do not make it too long or too loose.

1–2. Come up at A and slide the needle under the ribbon to smooth it; go down at B. Make sure the ribbon lies flat and is not twisted.

STRAIGHT STITCH—BUD

1–2. While keeping the ribbon flat, come up at A and go down at B. Come up at C and go down at D, creating a padded straight stitch; do not pull the ribbon tight.

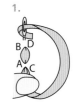

3. Using floss or 2mm ribbon, form the leaves and stem with a fly stitch (page 66).

STRAIGHT STITCH—ROSE

1. For the rose center, come up at A, go down at B, come up at C, go down at D, come up at E, and go down at F.

2–3. Circle the center with 6 backstitches (page 41). Overlap the joining petal points of the first round with a second round of backstitches.

TUBE ROSE

Thread a needle with a fine thread to match the color of the ribbon. Make a firm knot and set aside. Cut a 14″ length of 4mm-wide ribbon and thread it on a chenille needle.

1. Come up at A. Hold the needle and ribbon perpendicular to the fabric. Twist the ribbon into a tightly twisted tube. Make sure there are no loose areas.

2. Hold the tube securely in the center with your free hand. Fold it in half. Insert the needle near A until only the eye is above the fabric.

3–4. Let go of the ribbon, allowing the 2 halves to twist around each other to form 1 large tube. Gently pull down and continue pulling until the rose is the desired size. With the set-aside threaded needle, secure the rose with tiny tack stitches.

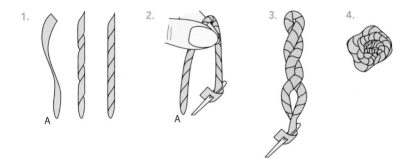

Twisted Loop Stitch

1. Come up at A, purposely twist the loop once, and go down at B.

2–4. Hold the loop in place and come up at C, piercing the fabric and the first ribbon loop. Use a needle or round toothpick to hold each loop until you come up for the next loop to avoid pulling the loops out of shape.

This stitch is good for plumes and frilly flowers such as iris.

Twisted Ribbon Stitch

1. Come up at A. Decide on the length of the stitch. Twist the ribbon to the desired tightness.

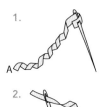

2. Keeping the tension to hold the twists, go down and pull through.

3. Nudge the twisted ribbon into place.

Variations

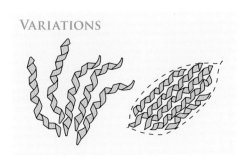

WHIPSTITCH—SINGLE

1. While keeping the ribbon flat, come up at A and go down at B making a straight stitch the desired length.

2–3. Bring the needle up again at A. Wrap the straight stitch 2 or 3 times, keeping the ribbon flat. Anchor the stitch by passing the needle to the back.

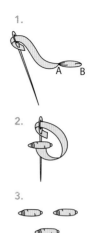

WHIPSTITCH—CURVED

1. While keeping the ribbon flat, come up at A and go down at B, making a straight stitch the desired length.

2–3. Bring the needle up again at A. Wrap the straight stitch 2 or 3 times while working toward B and keeping the ribbon flat. Crowd the stitch so that it will curve. Repeat the wraps, working toward A. Anchor the stitch by passing the needle to the back.

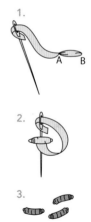

OTHER RIBBON TECHNIQUES

CHRISTINE'S BLOSSOMS

A lovely little blossom was created by Christine Simpson of Perth, Australia. They are a bit fiddly but well worth the effort.

1. Use 3mm-wide satin ribbon, matching thread, and a fine needle. Start running stitches (page 81) at A and create ½″-wide arches. Make sure the thread loops over the edges at points B, C, and D.

2–3. Finish at point E and gently gather. Four little petals will form. Join the edges and sew them in place. Add a bead to the center if you like.

1.

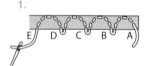

2.

3.

CONCERTINA ROSE

1. Thread the needle with matching thread and knot the end. Using a long length of ⅜″-wide satin or firm ribbon, fold the ribbon at a right angle 5″ from one end.

1.

2. Fold the horizontal section of the ribbon up and over and to the left. Fold the ribbon up and over from the bottom. The folds will take on a square look. Keep folding from right to left, top to bottom, left to right, and bottom to top until the 5″ is used up.

continued on page 113

3–5. Grasp both ends in one hand and pull gently down on the long end until a rose is formed. With the knotted thread, go through the center, come back up and down again. Tightly wrap the ribbon ends at the base. Make a knot and cut the thread, leaving a 6″ tail of thread for attaching the rose later. Trim the ribbon ends as closely as possible without cutting the thread.

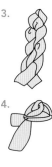

ELLY'S WIRE RIBBON PANSY

Elly Sienkiewicz, author of many best-selling books including *Romancing Ribbons into Flowers*, shares her wire ribbon pansy with us.

1. Cut 2 lengths of ribbon, each 4 ribbon widths long. Overlap the ribbon at a 90° angle. Sew a running stitch (page 81) along the ribbons as shown.

2. Gather the ribbons to form a back petal. Wrap the thread around the ribbon ends to secure. Repeat the process for a second back petal.

3. Cut 1 length of ribbon 12 ribbon widths long and fold into 3 equal sections. Sew a running stitch along the ribbon edge.

4. Gather the ribbon to form 3 front petals. Wrap the thread around the ribbon ends to secure the center.

5. Secure the 2 back petals to the front 3-petal unit to create the pansy. Add a bead for the center or use ribbon or embroidery thread to cover the pansy center.

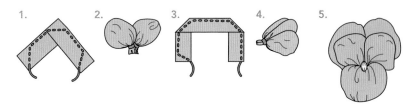

FIVE-PETAL GATHERED FLOWER

The size of this 5-sided flower will vary depending on the width of the ribbon and the width of the 5 intervals.

1. For ⅝″-wide ribbon, cut a length 7⅜″ long. Mark at 1⅜″ intervals. Using a running stitch (page 81), sew 5 half circles. Make sure the thread loops over the ribbon edge at the bottom of each half circle. This ensures that the ribbon will gather up easily.

2–3. Gently pull the running-stitch thread, gathering the ribbon into 5 petals. When the petals are pulled into place, sew the 2 ends together and trim away any excess. Add French knots (page 68) or pistil stitches (page 79) to the center.

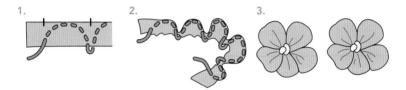

FOLDED RIBBON ROSE

These can be made from various widths and types of ribbon. The size of the rose is determined by the width of the ribbon and the number of folds.

1. Make a 90°-angled fold on the right end of the ribbon, about 1″ from the end.

2. Roll firmly for 3 turns to form the center of the rose.

3. Stitch firmly at the lower edge of the roll, through all the layers of ribbon. Let the needle and thread dangle.

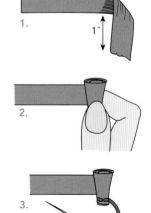

continued on page 115

4. With your thumb and forefinger, fold the top edge of the ribbon back and down so the fold lies on top of the twist.

5. Wrap the ribbon around the center to form the first petal. Pick up the dangling needle and anchor the folded petal, piercing all layers of ribbon. Pull tight and make a knot. Let the needle dangle.

6. Begin the second petal, using your thumb and forefinger. Fold the top edge back and down as before and secure. Continue around, securing, folding, wrapping, and stitching until the rose is the desired size (3 or 4 more rounds). Clip the ends and sew in place.

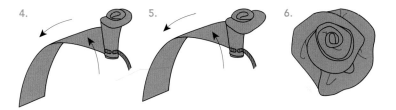

FOLDED ROSEBUD

The folded rosebud is simply the rolled center and 1 petal of the folded rose.

1. Make a 90° angle 1″ from the end of a piece of ribbon.

2. Make 3 tight rolls. Stitch to anchor tightly at the base. Make a petal by folding the ribbon back and down.

3. Wrap this petal around the rolled ribbon, angling the petal toward the base of the bud. Stitch at the base and secure.

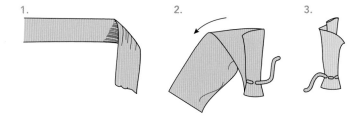

Free-Form Flower

Use narrow ribbon, ⅛″ to ¼″ wide, cut in 3″ lengths for tiny flowers; or use wider, ½″- to 1″-wide ribbon cut in 4″ lengths for larger flowers.

1. Fold both ends under and baste along one long edge.

2. Pull the thread to gather tightly and knot the thread ends. Stitch the folded ribbon ends together. Leave a thread tail to attach the flower later.

Japanese Wire Ribbon Bud

Use a wide, wire-edged ombré ribbon.

1. Cut a piece of ribbon the exact length of the ribbon width to form a square.

2. Fold the piece into a triangle, with the fold on top.

3. Fold one wing tightly into the center.

4. Fold the other wing backward and down, keeping it rather loose, to form a bud or lily shape.

5–6. Using a needle and strong thread, pierce the bottom and wrap tightly. Make a knot. Trim off the excess ribbon and sew the bud in place.

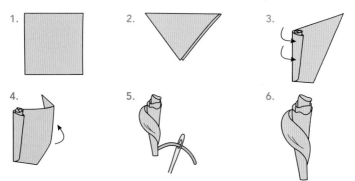

LEAVES—RIBBON

Depending on the size of the ribbon, these leaves can be ⅛″ to 2″ wide.

1. Cut a length of ribbon 3 ribbon widths long. Fold diagonally into a point. Baste along the wide edge.

2–3. Pull the thread to gather. Make a knot and leave a tail for tacking. Note: Tack leaves down before flowers.

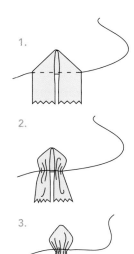

MOKUBA RIBBON FLOWER

Mr. Watanabe, owner of Mokuba Ribbons, makes this little flower using only a flame and 1½″ of Mokuba picot-edge polyester ombré ribbon.

1. Cut a 1½″ length of Mokuba picot-edge polyester ombré ribbon. Burn one cut end with a flame. It will have a hard, melted edge.

2. Unravel the widthwise thread on the unburned end to make a fringe.

3. Decide if the flower will have a light or dark center. Holding the ribbon loosely, pull the outside vertical thread of the dark or light side until that edge is gathered tightly. Holding the gathered edge, burn the raw edge to melt the threads together and hold the gathered edge.

4–5. Let one end overlap the other to form a small, cupped flower. With matching thread, sew the flower in place. Make sure to leave the outer edges free. Fill in the center with beads or French knots (page 68).

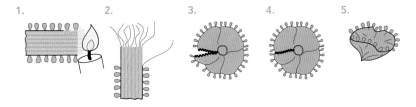

VICTORIAN VELVET PANSIES

Years ago I bought a Victorian pillow top covered with velvet pansies. I've used the designs on many projects and for book covers, but more than that, I've enjoyed making them.

1. Choose low-nap velvet or panné velvet ribbon or fabric. Cut the petal shapes (they can be painted later for more detail). Back the petal pieces with fusible web.

2. Place the pieces in order from 1 to 4, securing each petal piece in place with tight buttonhole stitches (page 44).

3. Keep the buttonhole stitches very close and vary the lengths to give a more painterly look to the petals. It is not necessary to stitch the portions that will overlap. (The dashed lines on the pattern pieces indicate where buttonhole stitches should be worked.)

4. Work the highlighted straight stitches (page 86); then the very fine, wispy, center straight stitches; and last, add the center. Then add the very fine, wispy, straight stitches on petals 1, 3, and 4.

Wire Ribbon Fuchsia

This flower is made with 1 piece of ribbon forming the pointed sepals and 2 more pieces forming the petals.

Sepals

1. Cut a length of ribbon 3½ times the ribbon width.

2. Fold the 2 raw edges to meet in the center.

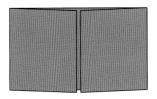

3. Stitch a diamond shape, making sure the thread loops over the edges at the 4 outside points. Sew the last stitch beyond the first stitch to close the diamond.

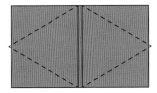

4. Set aside.

Petals

NARROW PETALS

1. Cut a length of ribbon 3 times the ribbon width.

2. Tack 5 stamens at the mid-point of one edge of the ribbon, staggering them as shown.

3. Fold the edges diagonally; then sew a running stitch across the center.

4. Pull the threads to gather and secure with a knot.

FRILLY PETALS

1. Cut a length of ribbon 4 times the ribbon width.

2. Sew the cut ends together with a running stitch to make a continuous piece.

3. Sew running stitches along the top edge and gather up tightly. Secure with a knot.

Note: A second method is to sew running stitches as shown. Pull the thread to gather. Overlap the ends.

PUT TOGETHER THE FUCHSIA

1. Tuck the narrow petal piece in the center of the frilly petal piece.

2. Tack the pieces to the center of the stitched diamond on the sepals with 1 stitch.

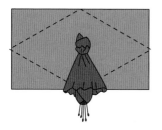

3. Pull the threads to gather the ribbon, forming pointed sepals and the tube of the flower. Backstitch and secure with a knot.

4. With a knotted green perle cotton thread, go up through the center of the flower and add a green bead for effect. Leave a length of the perle thread.

Sepal
Petals
Stamens

ADVICE FOR LEFT-HANDERS

This section contains some of the basic stitches written specifically for left-handers, plus some hints on how to use right-handed instructions.

IF YOU WANT TO TRY OTHER STITCHES NOT SHOWN IN THIS SECTION, TRY:

- holding the book upside down
- looking at the illustrations in a mirror
- taking a photo of the illustrations and using a photo-editing program to flip or mirror the image

After the needle is inserted into the fabric, use the middle finger of your right hand at the back of the fabric to help guide the needle to the front of the fabric. When the needle tip appears on the fabric surface, you can easily grasp it with your left hand to continue to the next step.

If you take a class, always sit right in front of the instructor to observe the stitches.

For more left-handed instructions, my *Embroidery & Crazy Quilt Stitch Tool* shows all of the stitches with both right-handed and left-handed instructions.

BUTTONHOLE STITCH

Work the stitch from right to left.

1. Come up at A, hold the thread down with your thumb, go down at B, and come up at C.

2–3. Bring the needle tip over the thread and pull into place. Repeat.

The horizontal thread should be on the seamline. Keep the vertical lines straight and even.

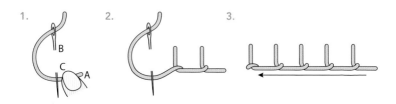

CHAIN STITCH

1–2. Come up at A and form a loop. Go down at B (close to A but not into it), and come up at C, bringing the needle tip over the thread. Repeat this stitch to make a chain.

CHEVRON STITCH

Work this stitch right to left along two parallel lines. Start on the bottom line.

1. Come up at A, go down at B, and come up at C (in the center of A and B).

2. Make an angled straight stitch the desired length to D, then come up at E.

3. Keep the thread loop on the top. Go down at F (equal to the length of A/B) and come up at G.

Continue working, alternating from one side to the other and keeping the stitches evenly spaced.

COLONIAL KNOT

This knot sits up with a little dimple in the center.

1. Come up at A. Push the thread into a C shape.

2. Wrap the thread up, over, and under the tip of the needle to form a figure 8.

3. Pull the wraps around the needle and back into B.

4. Hold the knot in place and pull the thread through the fabric.

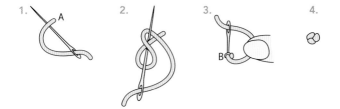

CRETAN STITCH

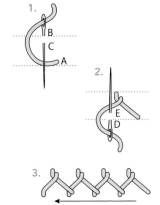

1. Come up at A. Go down at B and come up at C, taking a downward vertical stitch, bring the needle tip over the thread.

2–3. Go down at D, then come up at E.

Be sure to keep the vertical stitches evenly spaced.

FEATHER STITCH

1. Come up at A, go down at B, even with and to the right of A, and come up at C.

2–3. Alternate the stitches back and forth, working them downward in a vertical column.

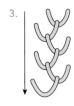

FRENCH KNOT

1. Come up at A and wrap the thread twice around the needle.

2–3. While holding the thread taut, go down a B (close to A but not into it). Hold the knot in place until the needle is completely through the fabric.

Herringbone Stitch

Work the stitch from right to left.

1. Come up at A, go down at B, and come up at C.

2–3. Continue working, alternating from top to bottom.

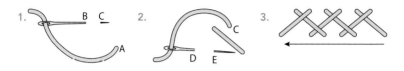

Stem Stitch

For a straight line of stitches, keep the thread above the line. For a curved line of stitches, keep the thread outside the curved line with the needle coming up inside the curve (C).

1–3. Come up at A and go down at B with a short, slanting stitch. Come up at C (the midpoint of A and B). Repeat, keeping the stitches small and uniform.

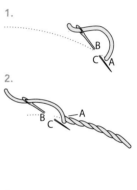

CRAZY-QUILT COMBINATIONS

BUTTONHOLE STITCH VARIATIONS

The following crazy-quilt stitches are designed to create beautiful, repetitive designs. Some of the patterns tend to twine and undulate along the seamlines, making a more open design. Imagine these as stems, flowers, and leaves when you execute these patterns, and you will be thrilled with the results.

Buttonhole + French Knot + Straight Stitch

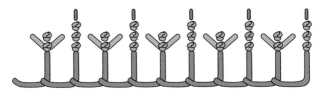

Tall & Short Buttonhole + French Knot + Lazy Daisy + Straight Stitch

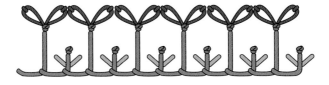

Buttonhole + French Knot +
Lazy Daisy + Straight Stitch

Buttonhole + French Knot + Lazy Daisy

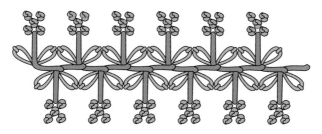

Curved Buttonhole + Lazy Daisy + French Knot

Curved Buttonhole + Colonial Knot + Lazy Daisy

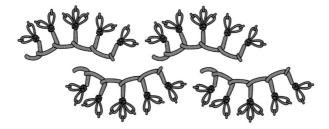

Curved Buttonhole + Colonial Knot

Buttonhole + Straight Stitch +
Lazy Daisy + Colonial Knot

Curved Buttonhole + Colonial Knot + Lazy Daisy

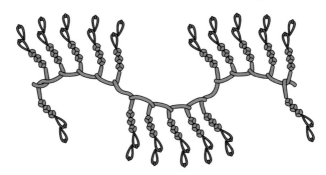

CHAIN STITCH VARIATIONS

Chain Stitch + Colonial Knot + Lazy Daisy

Chain Stitch + French Knot

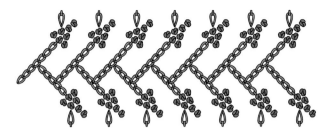

Chain Stitch + French Knot + Lazy Daisy

Chain Stitch + French Knot + Lazy Daisy

Chain Stitch + French Knot

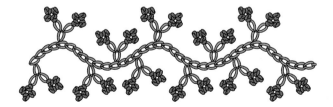

Chain Stitch + French Knot + Straight Stitch

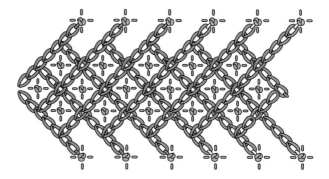

Chain Stitch + Colonial Knot + Lazy Daisy

Chain Stitch + Straight Stitch + French Knot

Chain Stitch + French Knot + Lazy Daisy

CRETAN STITCH VARIATIONS

Cretan Stitch + French Knot +
Lazy Daisy + Straight Stitch

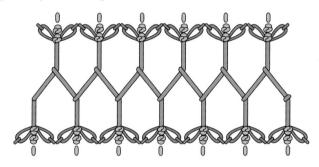

Cretan Stitch + French Knot + Lazy Daisy

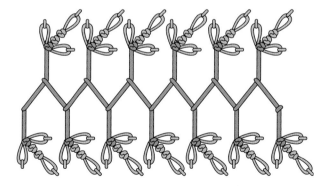

Cretan Stitch + Lazy Daisy + French Knot

Cretan Stitch + Lazy Daisy + French Knot

Cretan Stitch + Colonial Knot +
Lazy Daisy + Straight Stitch

Slanted Cretan Stitch + Straight Stitch +
Colonial Knot + Lazy Daisy

Cretan Stitch + Colonial Knot +
Lazy Daisy + Straight Stitch

FAN VARIATIONS

Lazy Daisy + Stem Stitch + Colonial Knot

Lazy Daisy + Colonial Knot + Stem Stitch

Lazy Daisy with Long Catch Stitch +
French Knot + Straight Stitch

Pistil Stitch + Colonial Knot + Straight Stitch

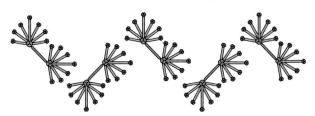

Lazy Daisy + Colonial Knot +
Straight Stitch + Pistil Stitch

FEATHER STITCH VARIATIONS

Double Feather Stitch + French Knot + Lazy Daisy

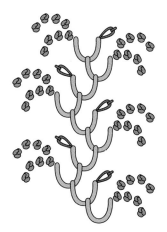

Triple Feather Stitch
+ Lazy Daisy
+ French Knot or Beads

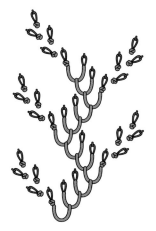

Double Feather Stitch
+ Lazy Daisy

Curved Single Feather Stitch + French Knot
+ Lazy Daisy

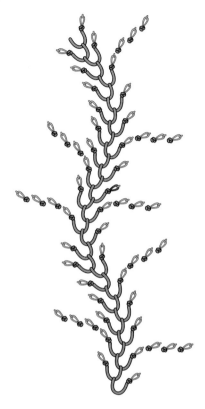

Single Feather Stitch + French Knot or Beads

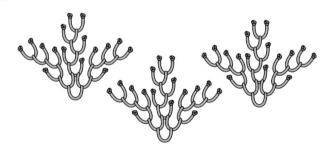

Chain Stitch + Single Feather Stitch
+ Colonial Knot + Lazy Daisy

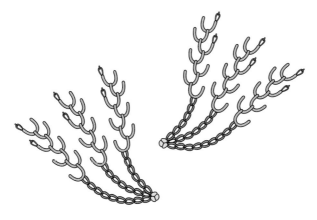

Feather Stitch + Lazy Daisy + Colonial Knot

HERRINGBONE VARIATIONS

Herringbone + Straight Stitch
+ Lazy Daisy + French Knot

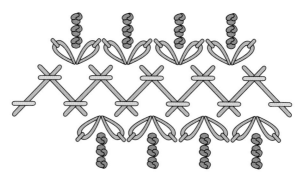

Herringbone + Straight Stitch
+ Lazy Daisy + Colonial Knot

Herringbone + Straight Stitch
+ Lazy Daisy + French Knot

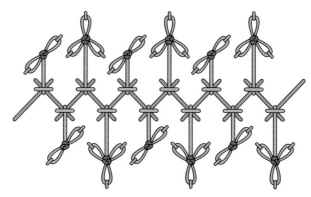

Herringbone + Straight Stitch
+ Lazy Daisy + French Knot

LAZY DAISY VARIATIONS

Long & Medium Lazy Daisy + Colonial Knot

Long & Medium Lazy Daisy + Straight Stitch

Long & Short Lazy Daisy + Pistil Stitch
+ Colonial Knot

Long & Short Lazy Daisy + Straight Stitch
+ Pistil Stitch + Stem Stitch + French Knot

Long Lazy Daisy with Long Catch Stitch
+ Pistil Stitch + Colonial Knot

Short Lazy Daisy + French Knot

Long & Short Lazy Daisy + Outline Stitch
+ Pistil Stitch + French Knot

Lazy Daisy + French Knot or Beads

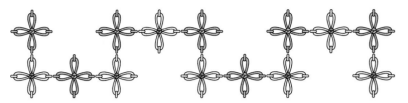

Lazy Daisy + French Knot

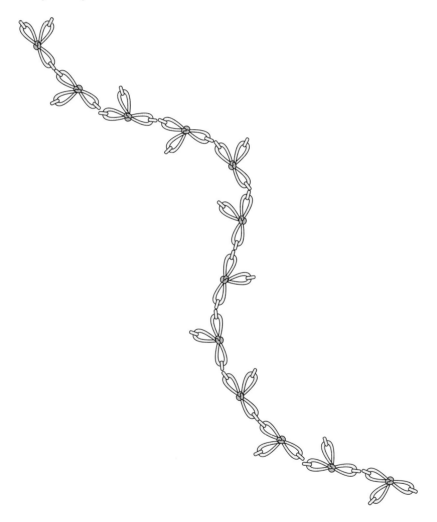

VINE VARIATIONS

Chain Stitch or Stem Stitch
+ Lazy Daisy
+ Colonial Knot
+ French Knot

Lazy Daisy with
Long Catch Stitch
+ Colonial Knot
+ Single Wrap French Knot
+ Chain Stitch
+ Stem Stitch

Chain Stitch
+ Stem Stitch
+ Lazy Daisy
+ Colonial Knot
+ French Knot
+ Pistil Stitch
+ Straight Stitch

Chain Stitch
+ French Knot
+ Lazy Daisy
+ Pistil Stitch
+ Stem Stitch

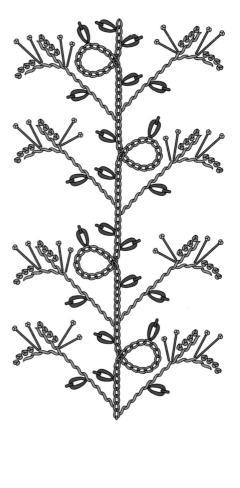

Decorative Lazy Daisy
+ Straight Stitch
+ Chain Stitch

Chain Stitch
+ French Knot
+ Straight Stitch

Semicircle Variations

Stem Stitch + Straight Stitch
+ Colonial Knot + Lazy Daisy

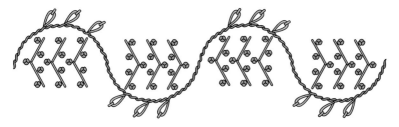

Chain Stitch + Lazy Daisy

Fly Stitch + French Knot

Maidenhair Stitch + Single Wrap French Knot

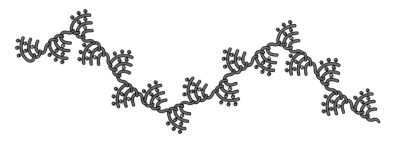

ZIGZAGS AND SQUARES

Straight Stitch + Lazy Daisy + French Knot

Straight Stitch + Lazy Daisy + French Knot

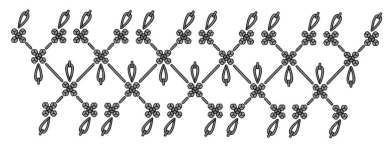

Straight Stitch + Long & Short Lazy Daisy
+ French Knot

Rosette Stitch + Lazy Daisy + Straight Stitch

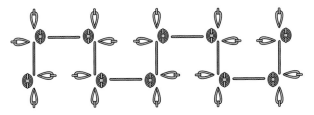

Straight Stitch + Lazy Daisy + Colonial Knot

RIBBON AND THREAD VARIATIONS

Ruth's Rosettes + Straight Stitch (ribbon)
+ Japanese Ribbon Stitch (ribbon)

Ruth's Rosettes + Straight Stitch (ribbon)

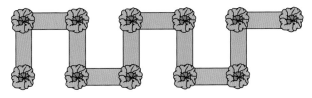

Double Feather Stitch (thread) + Japanese Ribbon Stitch (ribbon) + French Knot (ribbon) or Beads

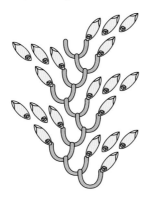

Triple Feather Stitch (thread) + Decorative Lazy Daisy (ribbon) + Japanese Ribbon Stitch (ribbon)

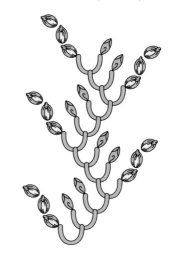

Double Feather Stitch (thread) + Colonial Knot (ribbon) + Japanese Ribbon Stitch (ribbon)

Double Feather Stitch (thread) + Rosette Bud (ribbon) + Colonial Knot (ribbon)

FREE-FORM EMBROIDERY

The needleart collages in this chapter are explained so you can see the process.

Over the years I have developed the confidence to think like a painter with fabric, threads, and ribbons. The needleart collages in this chapter are explained so you can see the process.

Although my work seems to be very free and easy, I do have a set process from which I seldom vary. No matter how hard I try to leave out a few steps, I always regret it, and it creates more problems. I have wasted more time waiting for inspiration or a good design idea, and it wasn't until I started to keep an art journal and store clippings that I realized that inspiration is 90 percent research!

I recommend having a definite idea, along with colored drawings, to start the plan for your project. Know the exact size of your finished project beforehand, so there will be no surprises. Before you ever put the needle to thread, be sure you have all your materials at hand. By having a sketch and notes on the project, you will have an idea of what materials to pull. (Perhaps you won't use them all, but the majority will be at hand.)

Remember to think like a painter, and that all your projects are a backward journey. You have to start at the furthest point and work forward. Yes, some of your stitches will get covered up, but that is part of the process—building forward. I hope you enjoy the following projects and that you will try some of them. Above all, relax and enjoy!

SONG FOR THE FRENCH ACTRESS

Crazy quilting is my first love, and I enjoy the challenges it offers. Some people think that everything and anything goes into a crazy quilt and that it must be very easy, but I assure you, it is not as easy as it looks. Crazy quilting is the most painterly method of all the quilting techniques. No patterns or templates are used in crazy quilting, and because the maker must think like a painter, crazy quilting can be quite daunting.

Crazy quilting is very process oriented, yet once you work through the stages, it becomes second nature. After you learn to think like a painter, everything from clothing design to quilting will seem a little easier. Read through Think Like a Painter (page 33) to refresh your memory.

Crazy quilt projects can be framed like a painting, and that is what I plan to do with this highly decorated square. This crazy-quilt collage features a postcard of a young French actress. I have a large collection of

7MM. SILK RibboN
Loop Roses
FreNch KNoT
CeNTers...

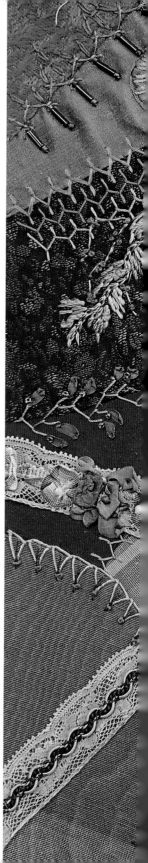

Silk ribbon embroidery makes wonderful surrounds for silk photographs and postcard prints. Choose colours to compliment the subject and crazy quilt surround.

antique postcards and photographs, more than 100 years old, and therefore copyright free. I scanned this photograph and made a sized copy of it in Photoshop that I printed out on jacquard inkjet-prepared silk fabric (the paper backing peels off when ready to use). I made sure to leave a ½″ border all around when cutting it out.

After carefully choosing my fabrics (I had to decide if it would be a pastel, dusty, or jewel-tone collage), I checked once again to make sure that nothing bounced forward too fast—in other words, that nothing was too light for the project. I wanted to make sure that the fabrics would not overwhelm the soft coloring of the photograph.

I also made sure that the fabrics were complementary colors so they would sparkle when used against each other. These fabrics represent the first color wash and will act as a background for the embellishments.

For this piece I tried to keep a soft, feminine theme, right down to the Victorian stitches, which you can find in Crazy-Quilt Combinations (page 126). Just remember that the focus is the photograph; don't let the stitching and embellishments overwhelm the piece.

tip

Use a good variety of solids, patterns, and textured fabrics in an equal amount of cool and warm tones. Remember that you will be layering ribbons, laces, and many needlework techniques over this background.

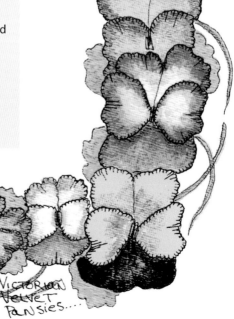

Victorian Velvet Pansies...

Buttons and beads mix well with silk ribbon Embroidery.

Cottage Garden #2

I created the first cottage project for my Australian students. It is a process project that begins with a painting on fabric and then a crazy-quilt surround, lace collage, pen-and-ink sketching, crewel embroidery, silk ribbon embroidery, Victorian stitches, wool embroidery, beading, ruched ribbons, fabric manipulation, burning techniques, buttons, charms … the list goes on and on! It is quite a list, but when you think of all the needleart techniques you've learned over the years, you probably know how to do a lot of them.

I take photographs of old houses and cottages and create watercolor paintings from some of them. I wanted to try painting directly onto fabric and experimented with different types of fabrics. I chose a fine-grade cross-stitch cloth because it was a natural cotton fiber and the small holes made it easier to stitch.

The idea of a crazy-quilt surround happened as I was working with a fabric painting and a crazy-quilt piece, trying to meld them into one project. I decided to work with a cottage painting fitted into a center cutout of crazy quilting.

Using a Window Template

Because I often frame my pieces using standard precut mats and frames, I work with a window template to make sure the work will fit when matted and framed. Sometimes I use a window cut from a large piece of template plastic or a purchased framing mat.

For example, when making Cottage Garden #2, I used both—I decided on a 9″ × 12″ vertical shape with a high horizon line to allow for more garden and more stitching. I cut a piece of template

plastic measuring 10˝ × 13˝ to allow for shrinkage and framing.
The opening was traced onto the template plastic and cut it out.
Using this I could make sure the painted cottage fit into the
opening. I also marked the areas for the horizon, walls, and path-
ways. I then transferred these lines and marks to a muslin base and
cut a window opening in the muslin base.

I decided to crazy quilt the sky and garden areas to create a painterly project. I chose small floral prints for the garden area and broke them into lights, mediums, dark mediums, and darks, in other words, pastels, dusties, dark dusties, and jewel tones (refer to the Montano Color chart, page 35). I also collected several batik-type greens for shrubbery and lots of solid sky-blue colors. These fabrics became my paint palette.

I started in the sky area with solid blue fabrics. Trying to use mostly horizontal lines, I crazy quilted very small pieces of various shades of the blues onto the muslin base, trying to create shadows and lights with the fabrics.

My next challenge was to make the pathway travel from the house out into the garden of the crazy-quilt surround.

After the crazy-quilted surrounded was complete, the opening was then trimmed and singed to create a drawing line. The painted cloth cottage was basted into the crazy-quilt surround and later secured with metallic running stitches. A few embellishments, such as the lace walls and some textural pieces

in the garden area, were laid in place on the crazy-quilt garden area. The small pieces of lace and ribbon added more depth and texture.

Next came the Victorian stitches. I started in the sky and used single and double featherstitches to cover all the seams with a fine thread in a matching color.

Once the sky stitching was complete, I went back in with watercolor paints to blend the trees from the cross-stitch fabric and onto the crazy-quilt surround. I let the paints bleed onto the sky fabric.

Every seamline in the crazy-quilt garden area was covered with a variety of floral-type stitches. To create a sense of distance, I kept the embroidery behind the brick walls small and delicate, using single threads. In front of the walls the stitching is a bit larger with heavier threads. The best example of this is

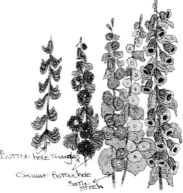

the pathway. In the background the stitching is small, and it gradually gets larger and heavier as it comes forward. The path acts as a V shape that draws the eye into the picture. It also connects the picture from the painted cross-stitch fabric out into the crazy-quilt section.

The stitching in the background is done with a single thread and tiny stitches. The section in front of the wall is done with thicker threads and heavier stitches.

The foreground area was embroidered with silk ribbon and heavier threads. This is the area to add wire ribbon, buttons, beads, pearls, and doo-dads.

On the Road to Seward

I am an avid photographer and keep a camera on hand at all times. I keep my photographs filed away in separate hard drives for reference. In the old days I kept my photographs in albums and filed all my research photos in file boxes under such headings as clouds, door, windows, animals, children, and so on. Well, I still do that, only now they are filed away in my computer or in a hard drive. It makes it so much easier if you think of your computer and hard drives as filing cabinets!

On the Road to Seward began with a June teaching tour in Alaska. We were driving down the road and came upon a lake filled with bright yellow water lilies. They literally covered the lake along with all kinds of bright green waterweeds and marsh. That scene haunted me, and I made several sketches for reference. When we returned home, I gathered up photographs and sketches for further use and filed them away.

I decided that *On the Road to Seward* would measure just 10″ × 14″ and would work up very fast. How wrong I was! I soon discovered that working small is more time-consuming because the stitching

has to be kept in proportion and all the fabric pieces are miniature and harder to handle!

I sized my photograph in Adobe Photoshop and made a copy using the filter Find Edges. This copy gave me lots of lines to trace in making a pattern for my project.

I cut a heavy muslin base, keeping a 1″ border to allow for shrinkage. The 10″ × 14″ perimeter was marked with a water-erasable pen using a framing mat. The mat is very important, as it will be used throughout the process to mark and check proportions.

Next I pulled the fabrics, threads, ribbons, and yarns for the project. I pulled more than I would need (for choices) and arranged the materials in two large serving trays. All the sewing tools were gathered and placed in a small dish.

Straight Stitches
Diagonal
Lines

Straight stitch
Branches.

overlapping
Straight Stitch
Trunks....

↑
Feather stitch pine
Needles - overlap.

Outline stitch
Chain stitch
Side by side for Trunks.

Chain
Stitch
Grass ➔

Loss Tree Roots

Straight stitch
grass.

Satin Stitch
Rocks.

unravel 6-12 stranded silk floss (variegates)
couch down with Matching Threads.

Because painting a landscape is a backward journey, the same applies to working with fabrics.

The sky fabric went down first, and then the mountain range. I worked in large shapes (some of them traced from the traced pattern) and glued them lightly in place using a glue stick. After I had the base pieces down (the first color wash), I started all over again in the background.

I completed each section, background and midground, before putting in the foreground where all the detail goes.

By now I had learned to work with cheesecloth, tulle, organza, and netting. I also discovered that I could hand dye my fabrics to get just the perfect shade or color for my project.

This little project was a huge learning curve for me, and I really enjoyed the process. I discovered that shadows in water can be achieved with layers of tulle and organza. Trees and shrubs can be created with ruffly pieces of organza held in place with an embellisher (felting machine).

Texture in the foreground was created using yarns, silk ribbons, and cheesecloth. Simple straight stitches and feather stitches were used to create the grass shapes.

Painted by Roberta Valentine, Giclee Print No Limit

JELLYFISH VIEW

This little project is a study in the basic stitches used to creating free-form underwater-scapes.

Creating free-form under-water stitches is just a matter of practicing basic stitches and becoming confident in making them. I spent hours perfecting the featherstitch because it was a hard stitch for me. Every time I started a line of featherstitching, I would have to refer to the diagrams! Now, I can do this stitch in my sleep and I can distort it into all types of shapes, from ferns to seaweed to branching, rosebushes, and so on.

Layers of netting, organza, and tulle create shadows and depth. It is quite easy to create shading and shapes with organza by burning the edges and overlapping. The jellyfish is formed using two layers of netting and manipulating organza ribbon along with simple straight stitching.

Even a small project such as this has a background, midground, and foreground. The background was formed with burned organza ribbons and netting. After the two layers were in place, the stitching could begin.

Straight stitching and some featherstitches in fine metallic threads were stitched next. These are decorative and hold the netting in place at the same time. The stitched seaweed shapes were embroidered next. I had to remember to work in layers to create background, midground, and foreground, using darker colors in the back and lighter colors as I worked forward.

Notice that the yarns and ribbons are used in the foreground. The stitches used in this project are net stitch (page 75), circular buttonhole (page 45), featherstitch (page 63), French knot (page 68), colonial knot (page 55), fern leaf stitch (page 65), pistil stitch (page 79), double knot stitch (page 59), needleweaving bar (page 74), and maidenhair stitch (page 74).

The silk velvet in the lower right corner was manipulated with needle and thread to create a brain coral. The stitched seaweed shapes were placed to look as though they are growing out from it.

For more information on making jellyfish, see *Free-Form Embroidery with Judith Baker Montano*, page 93.

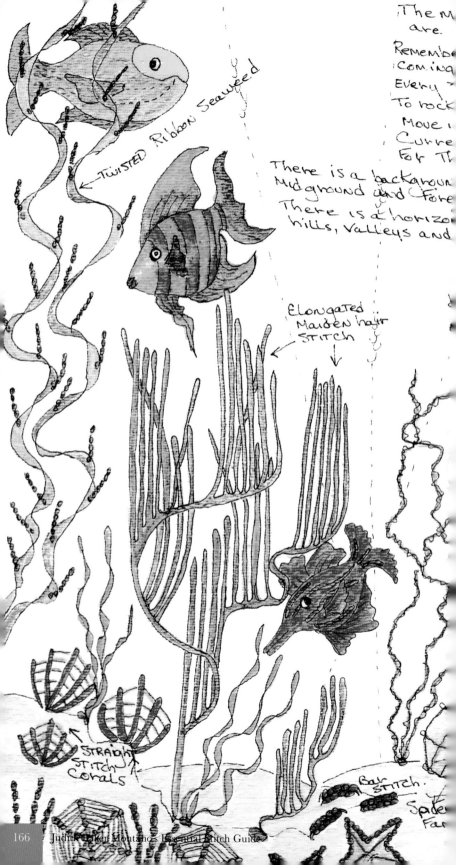

Twisted Ribbon Seaweed

The m
are.

Rememb
coming
Every
To rock

Move
Curre
For Th

There is a backgroun
Midground and Fore
There is a horizo
hills, valleys and

Elongated
Maiden hair
Stitch

Straight
Stitch
Corals

Bar
Stitch.

Spider
Far

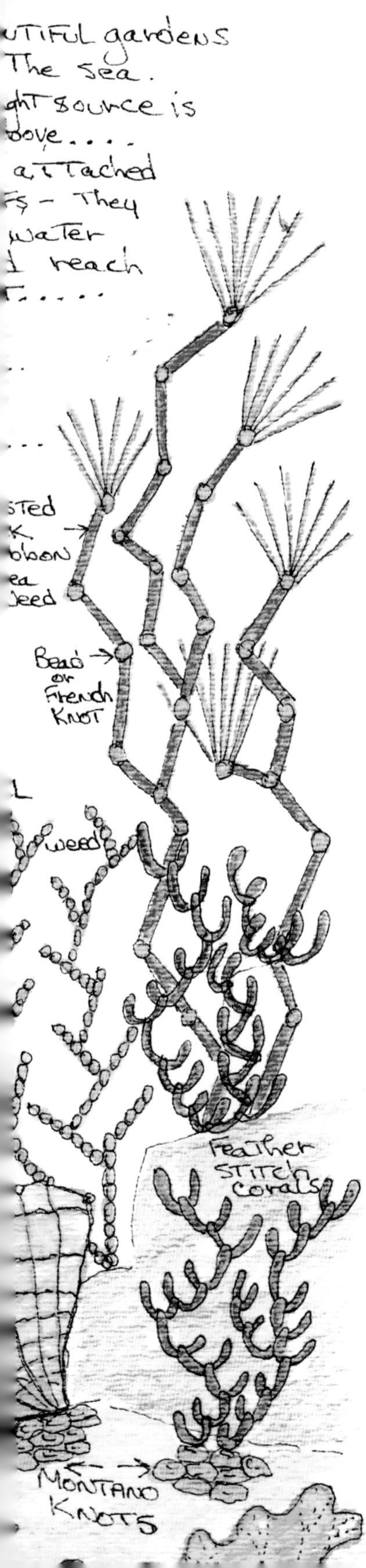

Handwritten notes (left margin):

UTIFUL gardens
The Sea.
ght source is
bove....
attached
Fs - They
water
reach
T....

...

..

...

sted
K
bloon
ea
seed

Bead →
or
French
Knot

L
weed

Feather
Stitch
Corals

← MONTANO →
KNOTS

UNDER THE SEA

At the age of 50, I decided to overcome my fear of water. I had always been fascinated with the ocean and seem compelled to return twice a year to walk on the beaches, head down, picking up shells. I took classes on scuba diving and snorkeling in Australia, and I have never been the same since diving at the Great Barrier Reef. I was able to glide among coral gardens filled with glorious color, and a whole new world opened up to me.

This is a detail of *Under the Sea,* which is the cover of my book *Free-Form Embroidery with Judith Baker Montano.*

In an underwater scene, you can use vivid color and create whimsical shapes that would never appear above ground. I have discovered that by using sheer overlays I can create a feeling of depth in my underwater scenes.

For *Under the Sea*, I used a painted background as well as burned-edge sheers to evoke a feeling of mystery. I was able to slip threads behind the sheers to indicate coral and seaweed. I used all the basic stitches shown in *Jellyfish View* (page 164), except that I took artistic license with the stitches and distorted them into organic shapes.

Once again the same rules apply to the underwater scenes: Make a background, midground, and foreground. Darks recede and lights come forward. Under the water are valleys, hills, flat areas, cliffs, and more—the only difference is that the light source comes only from above.

All the stitches used are basic ones that have been manipulated and twisted into distorted shapes. Don't be afraid to experiment with various threads. Split some threads to see if they will hold up with stitching. Try to unravel some tightly twisted threads. I do this all the time with fine cord or buttonhole threads. A tight twist has three fine threads, and I unravel them to use for fine background work. This gives me the choice of three widths—one thread, two threads, and three threads.

KAUAI, HAWAII

I often like to commemorate a trip or holiday with something other than a photograph or one more dust-catcher souvenir. A few years ago I was invited to teach on a fourteen-day cruise to Mexico and Hawaii. I decided to combine the idea of postcards and photographs into small free-form seascapes that could be framed like a painting. I worked from various postcards and magazine pictures to create small watercolor paintings of destination bays and coves. I chose 8″ × 10″ as the basic size because the mats and frames are readily available in that size.

After I completed the water-color paintings, I scanned them into the computer and used Adobe Photoshop for color adjustments and sizing. I placed the watercolor paintings on a lightbox and traced the specific shapes with a black marking pen. I now had 8″ × 10″ patterns and used them to trace the lines with water-erasable pen to the muslin base. I cut the muslin base with a 1″ border to allow for shrinkage and framing.

Because I was working on a small surface, I tried to keep the shapes simplified and limited the stitches to very basic ones.

Judith Baker Montano's Essential Stitch Guide

It is amazing to see what can be created with just the featherstitch (page 63), lazy daisy (page 70), straight stitch (page 86), twisted chain stitch (page 52), and a few French knots (page 68).

Perhaps this will encourage you to look through those wonderful holiday photographs with renewed interest. You just might find a photograph with a definite background, midground, and foreground that could be made into a fabric painting. While you're looking through those photographs, watch for any that could be turned into silk prints to be used in a crazy-quilt project.

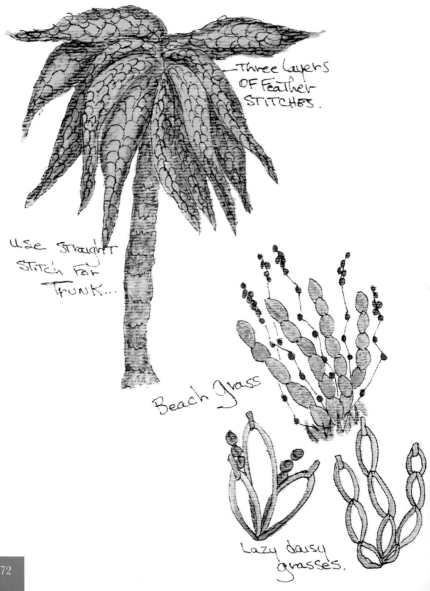

Three layers of feather stitches.

Use straight stitch for trunk...

Beach grass

Lazy daisy grasses.

She sells Seashells at The Sea shore....

Use Chain and Satin Stitch For Sea shells

Beach Rocks

straight stitches

French Knots

STRAIGHT STITCH

Chain Stitch

ODE TO PALOMA

I made this crazy-quilt wallhanging in honor of my youngest granddaughter, Paloma. Her name means "little dove," and I wanted to incorporate vintage dove paintings and photographs into the quilt. I went online to check for free downloads of vintage prints and came up with lots of choices.

I was surprised to learn that there are many different types of doves from all over the world, including Australia.

I sized the prints at 4½″ × 6″ to fit into a 10″ × 12″ crazy-quilt surround and printed them onto silk fabric. I chose to work in medium dusties, using rose and teal as the complementary colors.

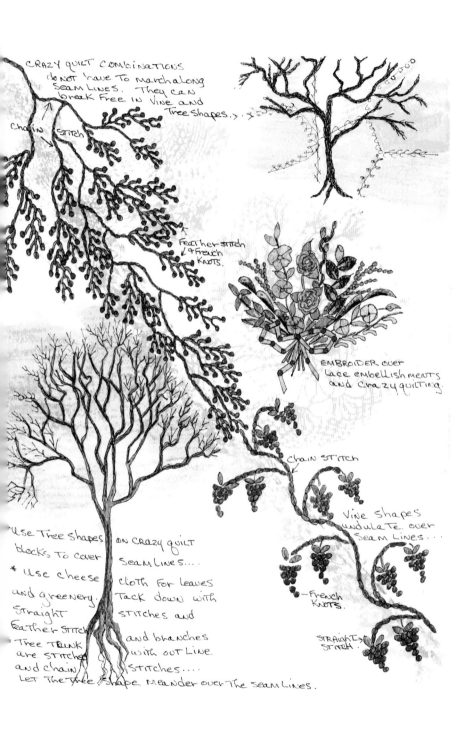

CRAZY QUILT COMBINATIONS
do not have to march along
Seam Lines. They can
break Free in Vine and
Tree shapes. ➤ · ≍ · ≍

Chain   Stitch

Feather stitch
& French
Knots.

EMBROIDER over
lace embellishments
and crazy quilting.

CHAIN STITCH

Vine shapes
undulate over
Seam Lines....

- French
KNOTS.

STRAIGHT
STITCH.

"Use Tree shapes on crazy quilt
blocks To cover   seam Lines....
* Use cheese   cloth For leaves
and greenery. Tack down with
Straight   stitches and
Feather stitch   and branches
- Tree TRUNK   with out Line
are stitched   stitches....
and chain
Let The Tree Shape meander over The Seam Lines.

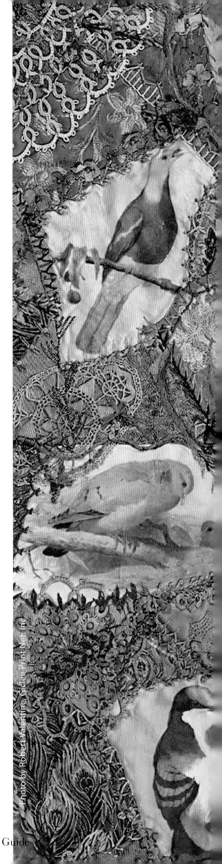

I worked up all nine blocks and then added vintage lace and ribbon embellishments to each. After the embellishments were tacked in place, I sewed the squares together in rows. I then embroidered each block and the many seams with a variety of Victorian stitches. I always work in this method because the rows of blocks are easy to handle and the joining seams can be heavily decorated. Also I can add a bit more lace and ribbons if I want.

After sewing two rows of blocks together I decided to embroider a large tree on a 12″ joining seam. The embroidered branching and cheesecloth greenery spreads out into the two adjoining blocks. I was so pleased with this effect that I added a large embroidered branch using my variegated threads. This branch kept growing and finally traveled through two blocks.

I enjoyed making this sentimental crazy-quilt wall-hanging, and I was actually sorry to see it finished. It now hangs in Paloma's bedroom over her bed.

Photo by Robert Valentine, Giclée Print Net, Inc.

Aguilar Adobe

I photographed this abandoned adobe in Aguilar, Colorado, and knew it would end up as a watercolor painting in a crazy-quilt cottage project.

Over the years I have developed more techniques to use in my crazy-quilt cottage projects. I started by collecting solid blue fabrics, with a slight turquoise hue to resemble the Colorado sky. Next I gathered all types of small floral prints for the foreground and garden area.

I made a watercolor painting of the abandoned adobe. I use high-quality watercolor paints because the ground pigments and sable brushes hold the paint better and last longer. Because I have done a lot of illustrating, I tend to use ink lines in my cottage watercolors for more definition and accuracy. I use size 01 Pigma Micron permanent ink pens.

After my cottage painting was completed, I scanned it into the computer and printed it on inkjet-printable silk fabric. This fabric

comes in cotton and silk and is attached to a paper backing to stabilize it so it can go through an inkjet printer. After printing, the fabric is peeled away from the paper backing and sewn into the project.

After completing the crazy-quilt surround, I carefully cut out an opening in the upper right-hand corner and burned the edges to give the effect of a drawn edge. I backed my silk print with muslin so it would have the same weight as the crazy-quilt surround. Aligning the surround and the cottage silk print, I sewed them both into place, matching up the horizon and pathway. I checked the outside perimeter using a 12″ × 16″ mat and drew in the outside lines with a water-erasable pen. Next, I used watercolors to paint the sky blue onto the surround and to dab in trees and shrub shapes, making sure they spread into the crazy-quilt surround. This helps to visually meld the two pieces together.

Working from the sky downward, I added the Victorian stitches. In the sky area, I used fine, similar-colored threads. I added lace to the wall area for texture and tucked in some organza and scrim behind the wall and in front for shrub shapes. I used soft, muted colors for the stitches in the garden area.

The tree was added to the foreground and made from twisted threads, yarns, and cheesecloth. Even the tree has fine, medium, and large stitches to create depth! All the large stitches and textural shapes were added to the foreground and finished with more detail.

decorated lazy

Lace ? Trim
for
Cottage Pain
Fabric . . . . .
Crazy quilt
Surround . . .
A Picture
Within a
Picture.

KNOTS Bushes

Curved whip STiTch Japanese Ribbon Leaves.

With Japanese Ribbon STiTch.

French Knots

SKY ALL The way Around

SMALL FeaTher STiTch in SKY Fine Threads.

Burned Edge

V shape PaTh Leads eye iNTO The Project.

181

Piñon Pines, Rabbit Brush, and Coyote Fences

This is a free-form stitchery that I created in a workshop with Jan Beany and Jean Littlejohn working from many photographs and sketches.

The piñon pine is a rather squat and chubby pine tree whose looks belie its very tenacious nature. It has to survive the droughts and harsh winters of the southwest all the while producing those delicious pine nuts!

The rabbit brush blooms in late September and early October, covering the countryside in a brilliant yellow haze. Rabbit brush has a sage green leaf with billowing plumes of tiny yellow flowers.

Coyote fences are so named because they are supposed to keep out the coyotes, but I have never met a coyote that listens to that old story. The coyote fence is made up of young tree saplings, placed side by side and lashed together with wire. The tops of the saplings are always of uneven heights, so it makes for amazingly beautiful fences.

Toss coyote fences, rabbit brush, and piñon pines together and you have the essence of southern Colorado and New Mexico. It was with these thoughts in mind that I started my project.

The background fabric was created with wool and silk roving carefully laid down to represent the sky and undulating hillside. The various colors of roving were crisscrossed on top of each other in three layers. When I was happy with the layers, I carefully ran a large running stitch in a grid design throughout the whole project.

Next step was to dip the whole piece into water. The wool and silk adhered to each other and formed a wholecloth!

When dried it was ready for the next step of using the felting machine. I took small pieces of roving to add to the thin spots and to even out the depth of the cloth. Next I added shading and texture, using various colors of roving.

Using coarse worsted knitting yarn, I cut small lengths to be used for the fence line. I tried very hard to keep the thinner, shorter pieces in the background with the longer heavier pieces coming forward. With the felting machine I was able to embed these pieces in place until I could embroider them down with straight stitches. After I had all the shapes and textures in place, I was able to start the embroidery process.

I used basic stitches for this project: featherstitch (page 63), French knots (page 68), straight stitches (page 86), fly stitch (page 66), and twisted chain stitch (page 52).These particular stitches can easily be distorted into organic shapes. I also used a variety of soft two-ply wool yarns along with heavier worsted yarns for the foreground.

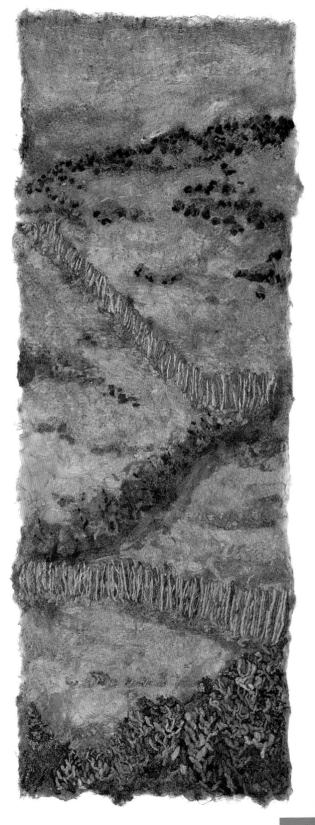

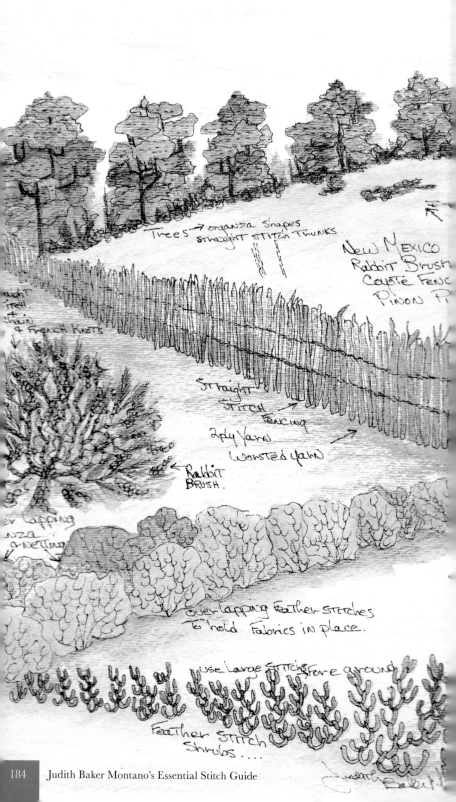

Trees → organza shapes
straight stitch trunks

NEW MEXICO
Rabbit Brush
Coyote Fence
Pinon Pi

Straight
Stitch
Fencing
2ply yarn
Worsted yarn

← Rabbit
BRUSH.

over lapping Feather stitches
to hold fabrics in place.

use Large stitches for e ground

Feather stitch
Shrubs . . . .

Australian Greenery

While working in Australia several years ago, some of my students introduced me to making silk paper—creating a pliable fiber with silk roving, fabric glue or acrylic medium, and fiberglass window screen.

(Instructions are easy to find on the Internet, such as those at meinketoy.com/silk_paper_inst.)

It is not difficult to make, and I enjoyed the process. After I had made a few pieces, I started adding other elements to the

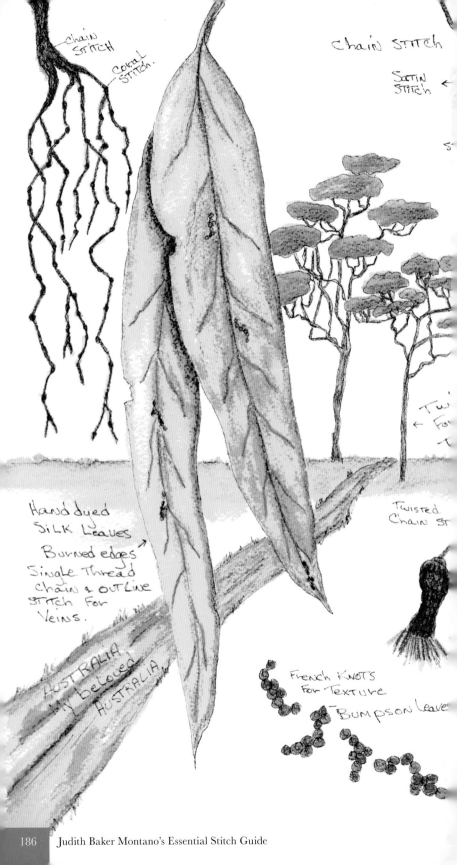

chain
STITCH

coraL
STITCH.

Satin
STITCH ←

Tw
Fo
T

Twisted
Chain St

Hand dyed
SILK Leaves
Burned edges
Single Thread
Chain & OUTLine
STiTch For
Veins.

AUSTRALIA,
MY beloved
AUSTRALIA

French KNOTS
For Texture
Bumps on Leave

ch
ril.

oth dyed green

Feather or Fern
Stitches
for Fine
Branches.

branches
atching

Chain Stitch

rch
ers

French Knots

silk roving such as bits of thread and yarns. Next I cut shapes from hand-dyed silk and rolled them into the silk roving. The glue and acrylic medium held everything in place.

I started out with a single thread from a fourteen-stranded silk floss to stitch in the gum leaf veins with chain (page 48) and stem stitches (page 84). These are the smallest and finest stitches because the leaves are in the background, behind the hanging branches and vines.

After the leaf veins were in place, I had to attach the leaves to the branches with stitching. I used two threads of the silk floss and used a chain stitch. The chain stitch was laid in side by side to change the thickness of the branch as it increased in width. The variegated colors also helped me to paint with the threads.

The vines are created with an elongated twisted chain stitch (page 52). By changing the thread type (from a fine smooth silk to a loose two-ply silk yarn, I was able to create a totally different look but still use the same stitch.

Featherstitch (page 63), colonial knot (page 55), and pistil stitch (page 79) were used to create the floral shapes. I like that the threads used in the silk paper are the same threads I used in the stitching.

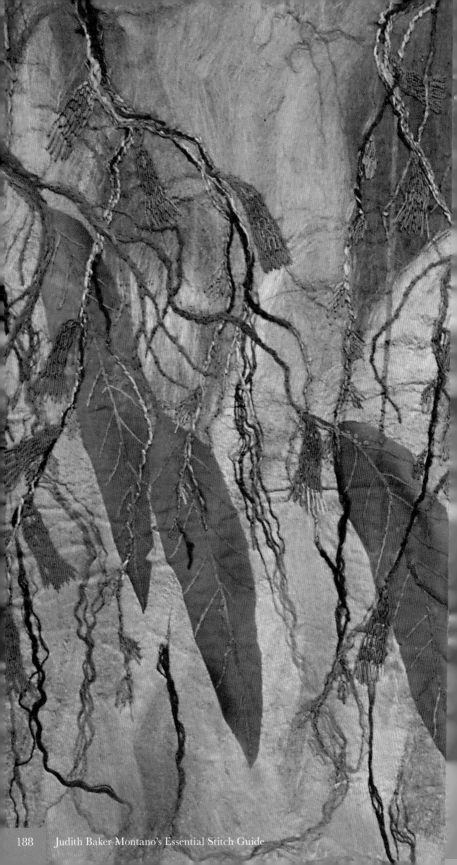

BIBLIOGRAPHY

- Arizona Native Plant Society. *Desert Wild Flowers*. Tucson: Arizona Native Plant Society (out of print).

- Barton, Julia. *The Art of Embroidery*. London: Merehurst Press, 1989.

- Beaney, Jan. *The Art of the Needle*. London: Century Hutchinson Ltd., 1983.

- Brickel, Christopher, and Judith D. Zuk, editors. *The American Horticultural Society A–Z Encyclopedia of Garden Plants*. New York: DK Publishing, Inc., 1997.

- Brinnon, Diana, editor. The Merehurst Book of Needlework. London: Merehurst Ltd., 1993.

- Campbell-Harding, Valerie. *Fabric Painting for Embroidery*. London: Sterling Publishing Co., 1990.

- Clayton Reddell, Rayford. The Rose Bible. San Francisco: Chronicle Books, 1998.

- Gaber, Susan. Treasury of Flower Designs. New York: Dover Publications, Inc., 1981.

- Hazelwood, Merilyn. *An Encyclopedia of Wool Embroidery*. Tasmania, Australia: Merriwood Press, 1997.

- Hiney, Mary Jo, and Anckner, Joy. *Ribbon Basics*. New York: Sterling Publishing Co., 1995.

- Holms, Val. *Gardens in Embroidery*. London: B.T. Batsford, 1991.

- Imes, Rick. Wild Flowers. Emmaus, PA: Rodale Press, 1992.

- Lampe, Diana. *Embroidery from the Garden*. Bura Creek, NSW, Australia: Sally Milner Publishing, 1997.

- Le Vine, Lilla. *Ribbon Works Special Edition Featuring Lilla Le Vine*. Gladewater, Texas: Ribbon Works Special Edition, 1998, p. 28.

- Morcombe, Michael. *Australian Wild Flowers*. Dee Whey West, Australia: Summet Books, 1970.

- Newhouse, Sue. *Creative Hand Embroidery*. Turnbridge Wells, Kent, England: Search Press, 1993.

- *Watts, Pamela. Embroidered Flowers*. London: B.T. Batsford Ltd., 1995.

- West, Deanna Hall. *An Encyclopedia of Ribbon Embroidery Flowers*. San Marcos, CA: ASN Publishing, 1995.

- Wright, Michael. *The Complete Handbook of Garden Plants*. London: Penguin Books, 1984.

ABOUT THE AUTHOR

Judith Baker Montano is a world-renowned Canadian fiber artist, designer, teacher, and author.

She is renowned for her free-form fiber landscapes and seascapes, which incorporate all aspects of art and needlework techniques. As the best-selling author of twelve books, Judith incorporates a unique combination of her photography, watercolors, pen-and-ink illustrations, and friendly prose along with her needlework designs and love of color.

Judith earned degrees in art and journalism from California State University, Chico. Upon graduation, she painted with the San Francisco Art Guild.

She began quilting in 1976 in Houston, Texas, as a founding member of the Kingwood Quilt Guild. *Pekisko Memories* (1982), an appliqué quilt depicting her childhood home, won Best of Show at the Texas State Fair, the Pacific National Exhibition, and the Calgary Exhibition and Stampede.

Judith's interests soon turned to clothing and crazy quilting.

Judith created "The Montano Center Piece Method," her signature machine method of crazy quilting. Crazy quilting became a constant form of expression for Judith, and this led to teaching and her first book.

Judith's garments, quilts, and art pieces have won design awards in Canada and the United States and have been featured in international museums and galleries. Judith's designs and articles have been featured in countless magazines.

Judith has appeared on many TV shows such as the *Carol Duval Show*, *Simply Quilts*, and *The Quilt Show*. She has produced several tutorial videos and DVDs, cards, and wrapping paper lines. She has worked as a designer for Robert Kaufman Fabrics, Bucilla Corporation, and Kanagawa Silk Company.

Judith was presented with the prestigious Governor General's Centennial Award of Canada in recognition for her work in the arts and representation of Canadians living abroad.

Judith and her husband, Ernest Shealy, reside in La Veta, Colorado, along with a menagerie of animal friends.

INDEX OF STITCHES